MINNESOTA

MINNESOTA

Text by Greg Breining

Photographs by Richard Hamilton Smith

PRESS, INC

Minocqua, Wisconsin

Thanks to the staff of Lake Agassiz Wildlife Refuge and to the caver, Konrad Elliot.   —Richard Hamilton Smith

Edited by Greg Linder
Designed by Patricia Bickner Linder

Published by: NorthWord Press, Inc.
                 P.O. Box 1360
                 Minocqua, WI 54548

Printed in Hong Kong

For a free catalog describing NorthWord's line of nature books, audio tapes, and gifts, call 1-800-336-5666.

To my mother,
who made the
sandwiches.
—G.B.

TITLE PAGE: Water lilies dot the shallows of a Hubbard County lake.
ABOVE: Cedar branchlets float on a pool near the Manitou River.
RIGHT: Afternoon sun illuminates forest in Tettegouche State Park.
CONTENTS PAGE, LEFT: Gooseberry River drops over Middle Falls
   on its way to Lake Superior.
CONTENTS PAGE, RIGHT: Northern white cedar root frames the
   Gooseberry River.

To Mom and Dad for always encouraging me to explore our world and follow my dreams.—R.H.S.

Contents

Into the Bogs

Canoe Country

The North Shore

To the Lake

Wild Rivers

A Gathering of Waters

Prairie Patchwork

Coulee Country

Introduction

Painted across a flat cliff face on the edge of North Hegman Lake in the Boundary Waters Canoe Area Wilderness, a scarecrow of a man stands as if in awe or surprise, with arms outstretched and fingers spread wide. Next to him are a wolf (or a dog) and a moose with antlers and a pronounced dewlap. Near the man's head are several horizontal marks and three crescent lines.

From what we know of Ojibwa culture, we suspect the person who drew these dark red pictures was an Ojibwa *miday*, or member of the Grand Medicine Society. He (or, less likely, she) paddled to this spot in a birch-bark canoe and climbed out on a ledge of rock above the waterline. He mixed red ochre with fish oil, animal fat, or egg and spread the paint on the rock with his fingers. But we don't know when he did this or what he meant to convey. From this painting and hundreds like it, some portraying fantastic myth-

ical creatures, it seems the painter had more on his mind than communicating with passing canoes, staking out turf, or even portraying the world around him. According to Canadian Selwyn Dewdney, who traveled throughout northern Minnesota, southern Ontario, and Manitoba to write *Indian Rock Paintings of the Great Lakes*, "To all appearances, the aboriginal artist was groping toward the expression of the magical aspect of his life."

Wild land demands a response. It's hard to ignore or dismiss the land as random. The people who lived here before European settlement fash-ioned their own pervasive mythology to come to grips with the country in which they lived. We still call the Manitou River on the North Shore by the Ojibwa word that means "spirit." The Devil Track River was named by the Ojibwa *Manido bimada-gakowini zibi*, or "the spirits'-walking-place-on-the-ice river." *Missabe*, as in the Mesabi Iron Range, was a cannibal who lived in the red hills of ore.

Farther south, the Dakota called one large lake simply *Mde wakan*, "spirit lake," and the river that flows from it "spirit river." French explorers chose the more worldly appella-tion Mille Lacs Lake. Settlers, by way of pun or misunderstanding, called the stream the Rum River. What the Dakota vener-ated, Europeans viewed prosaically.

Plains bison hunters, perhaps direct ancestors of the Dakota, incised a flat rock outcrop of Sioux quartzite in south-western Minnesota with nearly 2,000 images, including thunderbirds and shamans. Surely these people sometimes trembled in the gaze of the unflinching prairie sky.

Landscape has the power to move even those of us whose religion and culture stand apart from nature. God-fearing pioneer settlers venturing westward onto the prairie built their homes whenever they could in the meager protection of an oak grove. Not only did the trees provide very practical shade, they also sheltered the immigrants from the frightening expanse of prairie space. It must have scared them— a sea of restless grass all around and an entire

PREVIOUS PAGE: Low water exposes a gravel bar on the Devil Track River.
LEFT: Baptism River plunges over 70-foot High Falls in Tettegouche State Park.
ABOVE: Ojibwa pictographs decorate an outcrop on North Hegman Lake.

hemisphere of piercing sunlight overhead, as though the Almighty himself were peering into every crevice of their souls.

Those of us who live in cities or suburbs often feel as strangers to the natural landscape and the wild plants and animals that once lived within it. We go into the country to once again feel rooted in the land. In a raging blizzard in Minneapolis, I have hiked into the gorge of the Mississippi below the Franklin Avenue bridge and sat on the shore, simply to feel the raw power of the storm in the most natural setting I could find.

LEFT: Approaching thunderstorm lights the sky near Faribault.
ABOVE: Bison occupy a prairie remnant in Blue Mounds State Park.

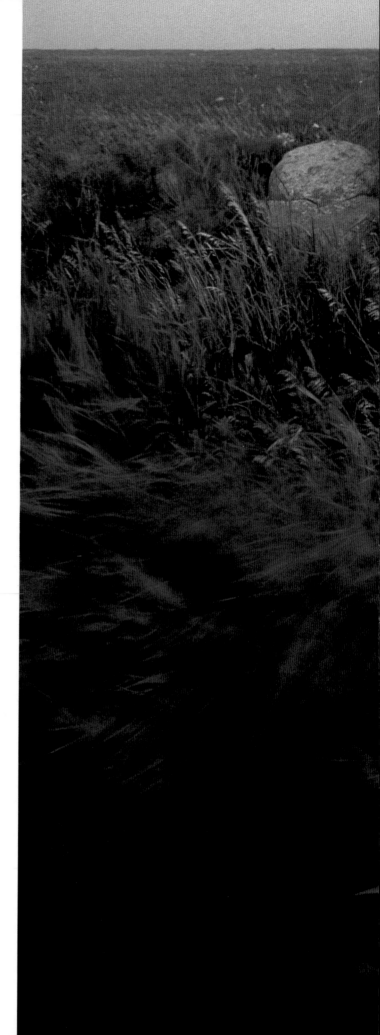

In Minnesota, the landscape takes many different forms. We're at a crossroads of North America—the point where western prairies end and eastern forests begin; where northern conifers blend with southern hardwoods; where recent glaciers ended and old-age river valleys remain; where falling rain drains north to Hudson Bay, east to the Atlantic, and south to the Gulf. The result is a stunning variety of landscapes. We've put much of this land to work in rather brutish fashion—clearing it, plowing it, paving it until it is scarcely recognizable for what it was. Yet throughout the state you can find country that looks as it did hundreds or thousands of years ago, when a gentler hand rested on the tiller.

Wild land has the power to frighten us, comfort us, give us strength. Like the Ojibwa *miday* who painted images on the cliff, we try to distill the multifarious elements and forces of the natural environment into simple images—be they paintings, photographs, or words. Thereby we capture the power of the land, make it ours, and better understand, perhaps, how we stand in relation to the world around us.

RIGHT: Goldenrod and prairie grasses swirl around a Sioux quartzite boulder in Blue Mounds State Park.

Into the Bogs

Canoe Country

The North Shore

To the Lake

Wild Rivers

A Gathering
of Waters

Prairie Patchwork

Coulee Country

The North
Shore

FISHING AT THE MOUTH OF THE BRULE RIVER on a calm morning, I can feel Lake Superior breathe. I'm standing chest-deep in the water. The incoming swells lift me to my tiptoes, then gently set me down as they pass. The waves are round and clear, a liquid magnifying glass, distorting and enlarging the rocks on the lake bed. I hear each swell rush onto the cobblestones behind me, as though the lake has taken a breath. Then comes the exhale, as water runs through the rocks back to the lake. Flow and ebb, in and out. As pebbles chatter among the boulders, I feel a sympathetic rattle in my own chest, as though I'm lying next to the sleeping lake.

Superior is not always so restful. I have stood in this same spot, trying to drive a fly line into a 30-mile-an-hour blow. At 31,500 square miles, Superior is the largest freshwater lake by area in the world. Strong nor'easters building across 400 miles of open water propel 20-foot waves onto rocky shore, launching spray 50 feet into the air. Boulders the size of bread loaves fly onto the beach. Superior's storms have sunk dozens of ships, from small fishing boats to the 729-foot ore boat *Edmund Fitzgerald*.

Superior seems pristine and timeless—a picture of purity and clarity in a frame of bare volcanic rock more than a billion years old. In its full fury, the lake appears invincible. Yet that is an illusion, as we have proven during the last century.

When white settlers first spied Longfellow's "shining Big-Sea-Water," they saw a lake of inex-haustible bounty. "Every river swarms, every bay is a reservoir of magnificent fish," wrote Robert Barnwell Roosevelt (uncle of President Theodore Roosevelt) at the time of the Civil War. But by the end of the century, log drives and sawmills had choked tributaries and estuaries with wood bark and sawdust, destroying habitat for several species. The lake sturgeon, a magnificent fish that sometimes weighed 300 pounds, virtually disappeared.

The deepening of the Welland Canal around Niagara Falls in 1919 allowed the sea lamprey to slip from Ontario into Erie, Huron, Michigan, and eventually into Superior. Attacking fish like a vampire, the lamprey made quick work of the native lake trout. Commercial fisherman Stanley Sivertson told me that in 1950, "One trout in the whole season fishing off Isle Royale had a lamprey scar." Seven years later, "I fished for two weeks [catching about 300 trout] before I had a trout that wasn't lamprey-scarred."

Other alien species invaded the lake through shipping canals and aboard the ballast tanks of foreign vessels—rainbow smelt, river ruffe, zebra mussels. We imported a few on purpose—namely Pacific salmon, introduced to satisfy anglers more concerned with jerking jaws than appreciating the resiliency of a healthy ecosystem. Over the years, Superior has become a goulash of exotic species.

Recently, we have tried to correct the course we have set upon. We've made progress in

PREVIOUS PAGE: Lake Superior casts a powerful wave against Stony Point northeast of Duluth.
LEFT: Framed by 1.1 billion-year-old rock, the Manitou River cascades into Lake Superior.
ABOVE: A migrating black-throated green warbler forages along Superior's shore.

re-establishing the native lake trout. We're combatting pollution problems in the Great Lakes, including Superior. Yet the horse is already out the barn door. Damage to this huge ecosystem is proving difficult to repair.

It seems to me, as I look over this infinite expanse of water and listen to its breath against the rocks behind me, that as a society we are

Above: Touching down lightly near Park Point, a feather floats on Lake Superior.

I PRESSED MY FACE AGAINST THE WINDOW AS OUR car sped northward along Highway 61. I was about 10, and I shared the back seat with my kid brother. He sat on the passenger's side, his window bisected by the ever-present line where Superior ends and the sky begins. I once read that George Morrison, the internationally acclaimed Ojibwa artist who grew up on Superior's shore, included a unifying horizontal line in all of his art because, as a youngster, that's what he always saw. Perhaps my brother, now in his mid-30s and a graduate student still, was lost in contemplation of perpetuity.

I sat on the driver's side. This side was more to my liking, with rolling hills of birch and conifers, soaring cliffs, and deep, mysterious river canyons that offered the briefest and most tantalizing glimpses as we crossed each bridge at 50 miles an hour. There was Encampment River, an amber ribbon trickling from a clay-colored canyon. Crow Creek lay at the bottom of a gorge so deep and forested I have never seen the sparkle of its rapids. The Baptism River flowed down a valley of grand hills and bald granite domes. The Cross River spilled over a high falls that disappeared beneath the highway bridge, a drawn white curtain that blocked my view upstream. And the Cascade River sprung from a black canyon, as though from the rock itself.

I wanted to find out where these rivers came from. I wanted to explore. Over the years, I have.

But many people never do. For them, Lake Superior is a linear landscape. Pinned between the lake and the swift rise of the land, they are dots along the line of the shore.

Break out. Get off the highway. Get out of the car. Go into the hills.

Drive up the Sawbill Trail, Gunflint Trail, or Arrowhead Trail, or any of the small dirt roads designated only by a number. A century ago, this was big-timber country. Near the headwaters of the Sucker River, the Brooks-Scanlon Lumber Company cut 33 million board feet of pine from a single square mile, a Minnesota record.

poor doctors—too quick to look for miracle cures, too willing to trust in radical surgery, too immature to recognize value in the natural health of an organism.

Loggers sent timber down the cascades of the steep North Shore streams, but the logs jammed in the canyons and splintered in the wild ride to the lake. Sawyers working the Pigeon River headwaters built a wooden flume to carry logs around the Canadian side of 130-foot High Falls. The flume's gray, moss-covered timbers are still intact, like the ribs of a dinosaur.

The vast stands of big trees are gone, but you can see remnants in areas like Tettegouche State Park. Follow the Superior Hiking Trail west from the trailhead. A third of the way to Palisade Valley, the trail winds beneath giant white pine, yellow birch, and northern white cedar.

If you're a hiker, you can follow the Superior Hiking Trail from Castle Danger to Judge C. R. Magney State Park with only a few interruptions. It girdles the ridge along the lake, rising, falling, and twisting like a goat path. Other trails climb Oberg Mountain, Carlton Peak, and Eagle Mountain. At 2,301 feet, Eagle Mountain is the state's highest point, less than 13 miles from its lowest—Lake Superior. Take the hike from Tettegouche State Park along Palisade Head, a sheer cliff that drops 200 feet into Superior's crashing waves. When vertigo subsides, look for the peregrine falcons that usually nest on ledges in the cliff face.

For another spectacular bird-watching site, follow Skyline Drive into the hills overlooking Duluth to Hawk Ridge Nature Reserve. During the fall, falcons, hawks, eagles, and songbirds of many kinds spill out of the northern forest and funnel

along the North Shore, passing the ridge in their flight south. Recently, in a single day, nearly 50,000 raptors were spotted from the lookout. More than 200 species have been seen. Common sense may dictate against staring upward with your mouth agape as thousands of birds pass overhead, but many people find the impulse irresistible.

LEFT: The Kodonce River tumbles through its mysterious canyon of rhyolite.
ABOVE: A sarcophagus of ice can't restrain the Pigeon River in its 130-foot drop over Minnesota's highest waterfall.
OVERLEAF: Blessed by a rainbow east of Grand Marais, Superior can quickly turn from calm to storm-tossed.

THE VERY BEST WAY TO SEE THE NORTH SHORE is to follow the streams themselves. They are rich veins of ore, the arteries of the land. They whistle out of the hills like the wind, diving into deep fissures and canyons toward the lake. For that reason, there's no better place than the North Shore to see waterfalls. Follow the trail along the east side of the Baptism River through Tettegouche State Park. It brings you

deep gorge, the other half disappearing into a pothole big enough to swallow a bear. Scoured by current and pebbles eons ago, the pothole must join a network of fissures and, at a point still unknown, return the subterranean stream to its mate.

One of the most beautiful river trails I know lies in George H. Crosby–Manitou State Park. This is a backpacker's place. Leave your car by the gate and go the rest of the way on foot. Trails lead to campsites scattered in the cool, haunted gorge of the Manitou River.

In winter, ice and snow fill the stream channels, and we have skied the rivers and waterfalls, dodging exposed boulders and treacherous open water. One cold night we camped on the Baptism. I have never seen a sight so colorless yet so beautiful as the frozen river— white moon, black forest, white river,

to the Cascades and Two-Step Falls. Poke upstream farther until you encounter High Falls, at 70 feet the highest sheer drop wholly within Minnesota's borders. Or walk along the Pigeon River, our border with Canada. Less than a mile up from the highway, the Pigeon spills into a mist-filled gorge, kicking up wind and spray that covers your face. Or hike along the Brule River, a mile upstream from the river's mouth, to the Devil's Kettle. There the river splits around a rocky island, half spilling into the Brule's

and black water running beneath gaping holes in the ice.

This stark aesthetic mirrors a stark essence: North Shore streams are as stingy as the granite and basalt upon which they rest. They grow fish not much better than the rock grows corn. But while the fish that live in these rivers are not large or plentiful, they are strong, and they fight with the power of steel springs. Many of those I catch are small rainbows, not yet ready to swim downstream

ABOVE AND RIGHT: High Falls' swirling plunge pool polishes driftwood afloat on the Baptism River in Tettegouche State Park.

to Lake Superior and complete their transformation to lustrous, silvery steelhead. But the most beautiful fish in these streams are the native brook trout. I take a few moments to admire each one I catch. It lies in my hand, small and vulnerable, as wet and cold as the river itself. Its fins are trimmed with a crisp line of pure white. Its belly is bright orange. So are its spots, which have subtle blue haloes. Its back is covered with vermiculations of olive and green, as dark and crooked as the shadows in which it lives.

ABOVE: The Manitou River races by boulders and birch.
RIGHT, TOP: Maples top ridges in George H. Crosby–Manitou State Park.
RIGHT, BOTTOM: In autumn's low water, brook trout spawn on streambed gravel.

One day I was driving down the shore toward home. To put off the tiring ride, I pulled into a wayside, where a tiny stream entered the lake. I had crossed this stream many times before, but hadn't given it much notice. Still, I had heard it held some trout, so I strung up my rod, pulled on a pair of waders, slipped a box of flies into my vest pocket, and began to look around.

As I ambled upstream, I flicked a weighted fly into runs and pools. The creek was unexceptional.

For the most part, it skittered over sheets of bare rock. I hooked a couple of tiny trout in small pockets of deeper water, but my chances of catching something large seemed poor indeed.

Walking along, my eyes focused on the stream, I suddenly encountered a 20-foot cliff that sprouted from the bank. I scrambled over and slid back down to the water. The river seemed to get steeper and faster. Around the next bend, the trail ended where a five-foot falls spilled into a crystalline pool. Should I go on? I cast into the pool. I hooked a fish and brought it to hand. A good omen, I thought. I climbed straight over the falls and into the canyon above. As I walked upriver, the cliffs on either side of the stream squeezed together like a vise. Rounding a sharp bend, I wasn't prepared for what I saw.

I looked into a gorge as if into a crooked tunnel with a string of feeble lights overhead. At the end of the tunnel, a 12-foot falls spilled in from the side and swirled into a big pool. It was riverine, yet subterranean. It seemed to lead to another world.

Here the episode ends. Not wanting to get drenched by pressing on, I retraced my steps. But I thought about that canyon through a long winter and spring, regretting my decision to turn back. Finally, the next year, I returned.

This time I fished little, making only token casts as I scaled the first falls and crept into the crevice beyond. I stashed the rod on a ledge next to the falls that had stopped me the year before. Then, reaching into the rushing water and finding a secure finger hold, I pulled myself up. My foot found a ledge, and I reached up again. The water sprayed down my arms and face as I climbed the lip of the falls and into the canyon beyond.

Awestruck? I can't think of a word to do the feeling justice. The walls shot upward and nearly met overhead. I spread my arms across the stream and nearly touched both cliffs at once. A crook in this crevice of rock hid the sky from view. Moss and ferns spilled down from the rim. Light drifted down like a soft snow. What should I do? Laugh? Cry? Scream? Pray? I couldn't decide. So for a time I did nothing.

Finally, I pushed upstream, climbing two more small falls. Ahead of me, the river split into three plumes as it cascaded down a 15-foot drop. There was no sound but that of the rushing water. It seemed, in fact, that nothing at all existed but the white water, the rock, and the pressing black shadow. The movement of the water seemed oddly important.

Above the falls lay yet another cascade, and above that, daylight—the end of the gorge. Digging my fingers into the rock along the falls in front of me, I started upward once again. But it was steeper and higher than any I had climbed. What if the next one was bigger yet, and I was trapped between falls with no way out? I thought of myself stranded in this crevice, subsisting on tiny trout and growing blinder by the year until a flood washed my pallid body down to the lake.

I let go of the rock. Then I crept back down through the deepest shadow of the gorge, crawled down the next big falls, grabbed my fly rod, and walked out of the canyon, the sunlight growing brighter and brighter like the dawn.

ABOVE AND RIGHT: Sheltered by shadows, the Kodonce cascades over falls before meeting Lake Superior.
OVERLEAF: Ice grips its shore, but Lake Superior remains open near the Canadian border.

Into the Bogs

Canoe Country

To the Lake

Wild Rivers

The North Shore

A Gathering
of Waters

Prairie Patchwork

Coulee Country

Canoe
Country

I LEARNED ABOUT PORTAGING AS A BOY SCOUT, on my first long canoe trip through the Boundary Waters Canoe Area Wilderness. Our guide was a big blonde college football player, nick-named Pheasant. Pheasant wore one set of clothes in the wilderness—boots, wool socks, shorts, t-shirt, wool jacket, and a broad-brimmed hat adorned with a pheasant feather. To portage, Pheasant stepped out of the canoe into water up to his knees, donned his light pack, hoisted his wood-and-canvas guide's canoe onto his shoulders, and shot down the portage trail. Accordingly, he had two rules: Never let the canoe touch rock; and make every portage in a single trip.

Second year, same camp. Our guide was Lee. A wrestler from a big Mid-western college, he was as short and muscular as a voyageur. Like Pheasant, he paddled the prestigious wood-and-canvas, which soaked up water and must have weighed 130 pounds by the end of the season. Lee, too, drilled us in the essentials of portaging: Don't touch rock, and never two-trip a portage. At each portage, he leaped knee-deep into the water, shouldered his pack, swung the canoe over his head, and staggered up the trail with a load that weighed half again what he did, as though he were some kind of oversized worker ant.

We mere Scouts paddled aluminum canoes. Truth be told, we could have dragged them over rocks the entire length of a portage and tobogganed down the steeper hills without causing them serious damage. But the guides made an impression, and we Scouts struggled the best we could, staggered though we were by 75-pound packs and 17-foot canoes.

For days we refined our portage technique as we wended our way through northern Minnesota and Canada. Indeed, we had good reason to practice. Soon, we knew, we would make a portage of nearly two miles. Every portage was made in anticipation of *the* portage.

Finally, the moment arrived. Lee shouldered his burden and disappeared down the trail at a trot. I shouldered my canoe and took off right behind him. My paddling partners took the packs and followed me. But we couldn't keep it up. With each bend and hill, we fell farther be-hind. For a while I could see intermittent flashes of Lee's shirt in the trees, but then I could see nothing.

We dropped off the pace and focused simply on following the trail, which seemed to grow steadily fainter. At a couple of points it branched off, and we began to worry that we had taken the wrong fork. Oh, where was Lee? Why did he go so fast? What if we're lost in the woods? Should we drop the load and look ahead for the next lake?

Suddenly, ahead on the trail, I heard grunting and cursing. Rounding the bend, I spotted Lee, mired to his hips in mud and sinking under the weight of his precious wood-and-canvas. Then, with a groan and tremendous curse, he heaved the sleek craft from his shoulders. It bounced off a tree, caromed off a boulder, rolled along the ground, and settled into the muck. Never again did the first rule

PREVIOUS PAGE: Sun sets on Crooked Lake, along the Canadian border.
LEFT: Morning fog settles on Kelly Lake, near the end of the Sawbill Trail.
ABOVE: A black bear cub peers through daisies.

of portaging carry the moral authority it once had. Now my rule is this: Never let the canoe touch rock—unless the water is cold, or the water is deep, or the footing is treacherous, or you're not in the mood. Then simply be as gentle as you can.

STILL, IT PAYS TO GET YOUR PORTAGING TECHNIQUE down. The Boundary Waters Canoe Area Wilderness is often called simply "canoe country." But those of us who know it would call it "portage country," for the portages open up the way to real wilderness. Portages are the threshold to freedom—freedom from crowds, from noise, from the wear and tear of many people upon the land.

As I plan a trip to the Boundary Waters, I lay out a map on the table. I feel the excitement of new country unfolding and run my hands over the slick waterproof paper as though putting my fingers on the land itself. I look for the red lines—the portages—that squirm between lakes. I compose entire routes of red lines and blue water, the rewarding interplay of portaging and paddling that will carry us off the heavily traveled routes into back country.

For those who aren't familiar with it, the Boundary Waters is a federal wilderness area of some 1.1 million acres, including 1,100 lakes of ten acres or larger. Motorboats are allowed on fewer than two dozen lakes. Through its history, it has been a land of paddle and portage. Routes of travel have always

run down the course of lakes and streams, interrupted occasionally by land.

In a way, canoe country is the oldest landscape in Minnesota. Formed by volcanic activity more than 2.5 million years ago, the bedrock is among the oldest in Minnesota. In fact, only a few outcrops in the world are older. Yet it is also among the state's youngest landscapes, one of the last parts of Minnesota to be uncovered by retreating glaciers 10,000 years ago.

The glaciers are responsible for this region's rocky visage. In effect, the ice sheet bulldozed much of the soil southward, leaving in places only raw, ancient granite and greenstone. In this cold, infertile environment, plants have had little opportunity to replace the cover of soil. Often I walk along a portage trail and spot a big pine tree uprooted and lying on the ground. Its shallow, spreading roots have peeled back 10,000 years worth of soil to

LEFT: Sunlight highlights a stand of aspen.
ABOVE: Symbol of wilderness waters, the common loon swims on a northern lake.
OVERLEAF: Snowbound islands dot Crooked Lake.

expose a clean sheet of rock. How thin is the veneer of the present over the truly ancient!

The scouring of the glaciers also created the lakes that dot the land like spots on a Dalmatian. The Indians who settled this country long ago recognized the value of these waterways. Over the centuries they had learned to build durable, lightweight, and streamlined birch-bark canoes. They had also learned and committed to memory an intri-

cate web of water that stretched throughout the north. When the French explorer La Verendrye asked a Lake Superior Indian named Auchagah about routes leading west, the Indian drew on birch bark a map that laid out lake by lake and portage by portage three routes from Superior through the Boundary Waters to Lake of the Woods.

Scottish traders and French-Canadian voyageurs followed these same routes in the late 1700s and

early 1800s. The primary route began at the post at Grand Portage on Lake Superior. Voyageurs lugged trade goods and 300-pound canoes up the nine-mile portage, which rose 760 feet in reaching Fort Charlotte on the Pigeon River. Up the Pigeon they paddled, to South Fowl Lake, North Fowl, Moose, Mountain, Watap. Finally, they crossed the height of land between South and North lakes and paddled down the Granite River to the chain of lakes that would lead them to the Basswood River. Their route determined what would later be settled on as the international border.

Between many of these lakes and rivers, the voyageurs crossed portages. Those who did not help carry the canoes shouldered 180 pounds of trade goods— more for extra pay. No wonder portages were dreaded. Voyageurs occasionally risked their lives shooting a rapids or running a waterfall to avoid them.

The men seemed to revel in the freedom of the open lakes. They sang to the rhythm of their paddle strokes, racing against other canoes for hours at a time. Thomas McKenney, who traveled with voyageurs in 1826, once asked his men if they were ready to stop for dinner. "They answered they were fresh yet," he recalled. "They had been almost constantly paddling since three o'clock this morning . . . 57,600 strokes of the paddle and 'fresh yet!'" Perhaps it was a relief simply not to portage.

ABOVE: The Granite River races over Little Rock Falls.
RIGHT: A pine tree springs from a shoreline outcrop.
OVERLEAF: Fog shrouds islands in Gneiss Lake, along the Granite River.

My canoe reflects the topography. For speed, its profile is aggressive, as angular as a cliff. With its long, tapering bow and stern, it slips through water as smoothly as a long rock point tapers beneath the surface, without ruffling the perfect reflection of sky. Made of Kevlar, it weighs only 36 pounds and rests on my shoulders as easily as a leaf on the water. Because it's light, it's also a bit on the flimsy side. If I grab the wooden gunwale, I can depress the Kevlar hull with my thumb. But once supported fully by water, the hull is tough and resilient, like bark on a birch.

As I paddle up to a portage trail, I pry hard in the stern, turn the canoe parallel to shore, and step into the water—with the aforementioned exceptions. My partner usually takes the larger pack. I toss the smaller pack onto my back, strap the canoe paddles into the stern with a bungee cord, and flip the canoe onto my shoulders. Then, carrying roughly 100 pounds—a light load for a voyageur—I lurch from the water and up the portage trail.

At first the pack and canoe pull at my shoulders, but soon I find my rhythm and the load rests easier. I begin to make time down the trail through birch and spruce, over gnarly roots and across rocky outcrops.

The scenery isn't much—not nearly as good as the view from a canoe in an upright position, with a sapphire lake and gray outcrops all around. This dense forest rarely offers broad vistas. Even if it did, I'm in no position to enjoy them. Instead, I walk in perpetual Kevlar shadow. My scenery consists of spider webs stuck around the front seat of the canoe, and the mud from our feet, plastered to the bottom of the hull. If I lift the bow a bit, I can see the heels of my partner's boots on the portage trail. But mainly I look down—dodging a root, stepping over a sharp rock, walking gently around a mud hole. Sweat trickles down my neck. Mosquitoes, knowing that my hands grasp the gunwales, drill my face. The sounds I hear are my own heavy breathing, the thud of my boots on the hard trail, and the scratch of branches scraping the canoe.

I once met three bears on a trail. Carrying only a pack, I rounded a corner and nearly stumbled over a big bear and two cubs. Miraculously, they didn't see me. I thought the sound of my beating heart would scare them into Canada. But they merely continued to forage through the bushes next to the trail.

I tiptoed back around the bend and thought a moment. Should I wait for them to go? No, that might take too long. What if I just walk through? No, that might startle them. Maybe I should make noise and hope they move off.

With that in mind, I marched around the bend again. As I saw the bears, I opened my mouth and, in one of the most ironic and stupid decisions I have ever made, chose to utter a noise I had made often in that stage of my life while playing with my young daughter: I growled, loud and mean.

Who would have believed that a full-grown bear could jump three feet in the air, spin completely around and achieve 30 miles an hour before touching the ground? But she did, and unfortunately, she was aimed at me when she touched down—30 feet away and closing fast. I sprinted for a tree and grabbed a branch. As I prepared to hoist myself up,

Above: Denizen of boreal forest, a spruce grouse takes cover in conifers.
Right: A waterfall joins two canoe country lakes.

expecting at any second to feel the hard grip of the bear's teeth on my skull, I couldn't resist one last look over my shoulder: The bears, all three of them, were gone.

THE PORTAGE TRAIL BEGINS TO TILT DOWNWARD. I lift the bow and spot that most welcome sight, a patch of blue shining between black trees. Stepping ankle-deep into the lake, I swing the canoe carefully

ABOVE: Red pine curls over Burntside Lake.
RIGHT, TOP: Early-season ice grips the shore.
RIGHT, BOTTOM: Bark curls from a birch.

to avoid trees and rocks, then set it lightly down. As we load the packs and push off, I take pleasure in the easy transition between portaging and paddling.

We put the paddles quickly to the water. A half mile away, a campsite sits on a rocky point. Every time we've been here, the campsite has been empty and waiting for us.

ABOVE, TOP: The federally protected eastern timber wolf is racing toward recovery in northern Minnesota.
ABOVE, BOTTOM: A snowshoe hare, which turns from tawny brown to snow white in winter, nibbles red pine needles.
RIGHT: Hoarfrost covers the ice on Fenske Lake, near the Echo Trail.

Into the Bogs

IN PEATLANDS, ANCIENT EUROPEANS SAW A realm of deception and evil. In sixth-century Denmark, according to legend, Beowulf battled Grendel, a giant who "haunted the waste borderland, held in fief the moors and fens." In old Russia, the *kikimora bolotnaya* lured hunters and travelers into the bog with its sparkling eyes and sweet song, then grabbed their legs from below and dragged them down to their deaths. The Irish called the flicker of burning peat gases that danced across the bogs will-o'-the-wisp and jack-o'-lantern. The Finns called these lights *virvatulet* and hoped to follow them to a pot of gold.

Gold was scarce, but bogs have given up treasures of a different sort. Throughout northern Europe, hundreds of "bog bodies" were preserved by the peat's natural acidity and lack of oxygen. These were no common burials or ordinary deaths. In many cases their hands were bound and their throats slit, as though these Iron Age men and women were executed, or sacrificed to ensure the prosperity of the village. Now, after 2,000 years, they have surfaced like tortured souls yearning for light and life. Writes Irish poet Seamus Heaney of the blackened mummy called Grauballe Man, discovered in a Danish bog in 1952, his throat slashed and his features frozen in a ghastly scream: "As if he had been poured in tar, he . . . seems to weep the black river of himself." Tollund Man, excavated two years earlier, lies in calm repose, bringing to mind a line from the ancient *Gilgamesh Epic*: "The dead and the sleeping, how they resemble one another."

So, with these prejudices, I stand ankle-deep in the snow that covers the Lost River Peatland, a dozen miles east of Upper Red Lake. In a way, I'm disappointed. Lost River seems neither sinister nor depraved. On the contrary, all is peaceful. Around me stands a phalanx of stunted black spruce as skinny and pointed as spears. A couple of ravens flap overhead. Paul Glaser, a University of Minnesota botanist who has devoted his career to studying peatlands, looks a touch mysterious, but hardly threatening. His wispy hair is backlit by the sun, and his long fingers trace pictures in the air as he explains how flowing water determines the intricate patterns of the bog vegetation. Yet his voice is as soft as the breeze in the sedges, and his checkbook sticks goofily from his shirt pocket, even though we are fully 20 miles from the nearest store. He looks less like Grendel than he does the absent-minded professor.

"These peatlands are probably the only real wilderness in Minnesota," says Glaser. Aficionados of the Boundary Waters Canoe Area Wilderness might argue, but he has a point. While Minnesota's popular wilderness areas are overrun by canoeists and hikers every summer, the state's northern peatlands remain unpeopled all year, as Glaser well knows. Once, after his truck slipped off a bog road made slick by spring thaw, Glaser walked 11 miles for help. "When you camp in these peatlands, you're on your own," he says.

PREVIOUS PAGE: The Red Lake River glides through boggy lowlands west of Lower Red Lake.
LEFT: Bogs, like this one north of Red Lake, were the source of mystery and dread to Europeans.
ABOVE: Tamarack, unlike other conifers, turn smoky gold in autumn.

A peatland is tough to appreciate. But after a while, you can admire the stubble of scrubby trees, the remoteness, and even the interminable flatness. Some, like Glaser, come to love it. "Aesthetically, I think they're some of the most striking landscapes in the world," he says.

Lost River lies in the bed of Glacial Lake Agassiz. Like all of Minnesota's large peatlands, it began to form in the wake of glaciers some 10,000 years ago. Glacial ice retreated and Lake Agassiz drained away, leaving a plain inundated with water in summer and bound up in ice in winter. Continual saturation deprived the ground of oxygen and the normal assemblage of bacteria, worms, and other agents of decomposition. Dead plants—sphagnum mosses, sedges, and the like—accumulated without fully decaying. The result is peat, a mucky and often spongy mass of organic

ABOVE: A long-billed marsh wren occupies northern
    wetlands in summer.
RIGHT: Beaver dams flood peatlands north of Red Lake.

material, the precursor to coal. The deepening layers of vegetation further inhibited drainage, causing the peatlands to grow across the landscape and form their own changing, organic topography.

Seen from the air, the subtle vegetational features—water tracks, ovoid islands of spruce, hummocks, and strange ridges and pools called strings and flarks—suggest fleets of battleships at sea, or the oil and canvas of alien impressionists. These "patterned peatlands" sweep across thousands

ABOVE: Subtle currents create ovoid islands of spruce and other features of "patterned" peatland.
RIGHT, TOP: A bull moose wades through wetlands in Agassiz National Wildlife Refuge.
RIGHT, BOTTOM: A dragonfly rests on a cattail.

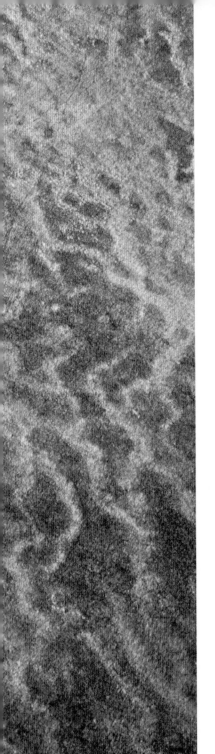

of square miles of Alaska and Canada. They make up most of Minnesota's six million acres of peat—a far greater acreage than is found in any other state within the Lower 48. Some peatlands cover many squares miles. The Red Lake Bog, a few miles north-

west of where we stand now, stretches over 35 miles from east to west, covering 83,000 acres.

"The two great environmental factors that control peatlands generally are water runoff and water chemistry," Glaser says by way of describing the

delicate intricacies that affect the formation of a peatland. He stands in a river of grasslike sedges sweeping out of a black spruce thicket. "The better-drained areas have trees, and the more poorly drained areas where water accumulates and rises to the surface have sedges," he says. Even now, in winter, Glaser's footsteps fill with seeping groundwater.

Subterranean rivers of groundwater, which can run as sweet as distilled water, create areas called

colorful orchids flourish in peatlands, including the ram's-head lady's-slipper, with its delicate pouch of white and blood-red veins. Several mosses and sedges grow nowhere else. Pitcher plants, bladder-worts, and sundews, some of them rare, have adapted in unique ways to this water-rich, nutrient-poor environment. Unable to draw sustenance from the acidic soil, they instead devour insects.

Black spruce, cedar, and tamarack avoid drown-

ing by sending out new roots from their trunks into the upper-most and best oxygenated layers of a bog. As a result, the base of a trunk may lie buried beneath many yards of peat. Because of slow growth, the tree may appear much younger than it is. "I've cut spruce that are only about this big around," Glaser tells me, holding his hands as if around the fat end of a baseball bat, "and I've counted 150 rings with a magnify-ing glass."

fens. Other parts of a peatland, fed by falling rain and melting snow, turn nearly as tart as sauerkraut as the water stagnates in deep layers of sphagnum moss. These acidic areas are properly known as bogs, though the word is often used synonymously with the broader term *peatland*.

The bog's harsh, waterlogged environment sustains a low diversity of plants. Yet many that survive here are unique or unusual. A number of

Wildlife, like the beauty of the bog itself, is often tough to spot at first glance. Yet it's here if you look. Marching along, we occasionally cross a line of grouse tracks. Sharp-tailed, ruffed, and spruce grouse all live in peatlands. Timber wolves visit the bog in winter, Glaser says. He often spots a few white-tailed deer on the edges of the peatland and a few moose in the treeless rivers of sedges.

In summer, several species of frogs, turtles, and

PREVIOUS PAGE: A mother raccoon and her cub scurry to safety.
ABOVE: A trumpeter swan glides over a beaver pond.
RIGHT: This red fox stalks a clearing in Agassiz National Wildlife Refuge.

snakes are common. Some small mammals also live in peatlands. Two that are particularly well-suited to this habitat are the southern bog lemming and its rare cousin, the northern bog lemming. These chubby, nearly indistinguishable voles dote on grasses and sedges and nest in clumps of sphagnum.

Some threatened and rare birds, such as the sharp-tailed sparrow, sora rail, great gray owl, short-eared owl, and greater sandhill crane depend on peatlands to survive. Others, such as palm warblers and Connecticut warblers are found in greatest numbers in bogs.

But some bog species have not fared well. Woodland caribou once grazed on lichen and sedges, their large hooves carrying them over the boggy ground. They survive in Canada but disappeared from Minnesota peatlands a half-century ago, as settlement in areas surrounding the vast peatlands fragmented herds and restricted their movements.

Minnesota's peatlands offer some surprises. Ice Age bison occasionally turn up in bogs. Once, as Glaser and his co-workers examined a core sample of peat, they found more than a yard below the surface a live crayfish. Nothing as startling as a bog body perhaps, but its presence was every bit as unexpected.

In 1975, in the midst of America's energy crisis, the utility Minnegasco applied for a 25-year lease on 200,000 acres in northern Minnesota, in order to synthesize natural gas from peat. The state set up a task force to identify peatlands that should be protected for their unique topography and importance to rare or highly dependent plants and animals. On the recommendations of Glaser and other experts, the task force picked 18, including Lost River

ABOVE: Double-crested cormorant skips across the water to become airborne.

and the huge Red Lake Bog. The proposal to formally protect the areas lay moribund for several years, but in 1991 the legislature added all 18 peatlands—about 150,000 acres of Minnesota's most pristine bogs—to the state's scientific and natural areas system. The peatlands, nearly all of which are state land, will be protected from logging, mining, ditching, and road building. In a way, it was protec-

tion by default. Minnesota's bog country was really protected by its own remoteness, inaccessibility, and simple lack of utility.

To see this country, drive north out of Blackduck on State Highway 72 and wander the back roads of Pine Island State Forest, Beltrami Island State Forest or the Red Lake Wildlife Management Area.

Try not to get turned around in a sea of stunted spruce with few outstanding landmarks to set you straight. And don't slip off the shoulder of some unmarked road and mire your car in peat moss up to the fenders.

If it's summer, slip on your hip boots, slap on some bug dope, and head into the forest to contemplate delicate orchids and feathery sphagnum beneath a cloud of hovering insects. Better yet, wait till winter, step into skis or snowshoes, and cross the frozen bog along an old forestry trail flanked by gloomy spruce.

Bogtrotting won't catch on anytime soon. Unlike Glaser, I may not be ready to pitch my tent on quaking peat and drink bog water to slake my thirst. There is, after all, nothing to do in a bog—no mountains to climb, no rivers to cross, nothing to distract us from the numbing sameness of the topography and vegetation. Yet, in the reddening light of a winter afternoon, I appreciate the serenity and enveloping solitude. The spruce and tamarack are black silhouettes, as black as the evil that lurked in the moors and mires of my ancestors. Yet I feel no trace of foreboding, only the power of a landscape that has changed little since people first beheld it.

ABOVE: A red-winged blackbird claims its territory among cattails.
RIGHT: A bare tamarack reigns over snowy hummocks in a bog in northeastern Minnesota.

Into the Bogs

Canoe Country

The North Shore

To the Lake

Wild Rivers

A Gathering
of Waters

Prairie Patchwork

Coulee Country

A Gathering
of Waters

Y OU'D EXPECT A RIVER THE SIZE AND NOTORIETY of the Mississippi to burst from its source in immediate grandeur. Indeed, we've tried to make it so, marking the outlet of Lake Itasca with a post that announces: "Here 1475 ft. above the ocean the mighty Mississippi begins to flow on its winding way 2,552 miles to the Gulf of Mexico." But in fact, the mighty river's beginnings are less impressive: It seeps unseen from bogs and springs and gathers up in several small lakes and beaver ponds before finally dribbling into Lake Itasca. The Mississippi's ultimate source is so amorphous that Henry Schoolcraft simply settled on Itasca, hiding his deceit with a combination of the Latin words *veritas* and *caput*, or "true head."

But once the Mississippi surmounts the crude dam of hand-laid boulders at the outlet of Lake Itasca, it begins to build its identity, thread by silver thread, taking in other streams as it riffles through wild rice and woods of pine, birch, and spruce, singing with magic to the countryside around it. Gaining in breadth and volume, it becomes, as the Ojibwa called it, "a gathering of waters."

The headwaters region was once big-timber country, covered with vast stands of old-growth red pine and white pine. Much of that virgin forest was cut to build our homes and cities, yet some remains. In Itasca State Park, near Lake Itasca, stand the state's largest red and white pines. Just down the shore lies the 2,000-acre Itasca Wilderness Sanctuary, a preserve of old-growth pine, where light filtering through the crowns of the giant trees falls on the forest floor as softly as your footsteps on the cushion of needles.

The river runs on, through state forests, Leech Lake Indian Reservation and Chippewa National Forest. Bald eagles are as plentiful in the Chippewa as anywhere in the continental United States. More than 180 pairs breed in the national forest, nearly six times as many as 30 years ago, before the ban on DDT and similar pesticides that accumulated in the bodies of many raptors.

Grand Rapids, Palisade, Aitkin—to recite the route of the river sounds like the call of a riverboat captain. A century ago, steamboats like the 140-foot *Andy Gibson* plied the tight meanders of the upper river, clipping the inside bends.

Brainerd, Little Falls, St. Cloud. Riffling swiftly though boulder-bed rapids and flanked by oak-covered bluffs, the Mississippi spreads out wide, already one of the broadest streams in the state. Despite its reputation as a working, polluted river, the Mississippi can be sublime. Below St. Cloud, its channels split between the Beaver Islands. Dappled with light shining through overhanging branches, this stretch is one of the prettiest along the river's course.

Monticello, Elk River, Anoka. By the time it rolls into Minneapolis, the Mississippi is a full-grown river, strong enough to carry barges on its waters and the weight of cities on its shoulders.

PREVIOUS PAGE: Fog fills the Mississippi River valley near Whitman.
LEFT: The fledgling Mississippi spills from Lake Itasca.
ABOVE: A broadwing hawk feeds a frog to its nestlings.

MORNING FOG, LIMESTONE CLIFFS, RISING FISH. THE glassy river slides beneath my canoe. I trade paddle for fly rod and lay a popper against the rocky bank. A smallmouth bass boils to the surface. A racing shell speeds by. A car clatters overhead. Streetlights on the frail, black arch of the old Lake Street bridge wink off as the city above awakens.

The river here has a hard edge. Spray-painted on a piling of the Ford Parkway bridge is a command: Spit on Authority. At night, campfires twinkle on the wooded bluffs and sandy beaches. It's a place for making secret deals—drinking beer, doing drugs, having sex. The river gives up a body once or twice a month. I counted ten one winter and spring in the small stories at the bottom of the newspaper page. One was a St. Thomas student who drove his car over the bluff. Another was a prostitute. One man was unemployed. Another was retired. One was a walk-away from a halfway house for the mentally ill.

So where the river slides between the twin towns, it's gritty and rough, and sometimes dangerous—the working river that people avoid. Yet it is also wilder and more beautiful than they realize.

In summer, the river bottoms billow with greenery. In autumn, the cliff-side sumac and hardwoods blaze red and yellow. The huge, dished pads of American lotus lilies choke the channels along Grey Cloud Island. Egrets wade the shallows of Pigs Eye Lake. Black-crowned night herons flap over the river at dusk. Fishing at the upstream end of town, I've watched an osprey plunge into the river for a fish. And paddling below the Ford Dam one evening, I spotted five beavers stripping bark from a tree on a sand spit.

A river's wildlife, especially its fish and aquatic insects, can tell you more about the river's health than a laboratory can. For a long time, the absence of fish and aquatic insects downstream of the Twin Cities suggested that sewage took a heavy toll. Winona State University professor Calvin Fremling

asked towboat pilots, lockmasters, harbor masters, and river residents all along the river to collect mayflies during mass hatches in the summer. His research, conducted from 1958 to 1969, confirmed popular belief: Despite the abundance of mayflies

from Iowa to St. Louis—nighttime explosions of emerging insects that buried bridges and roads beneath tons of slippery corpses—mayflies were conspicuously absent between the Twin Cities and Lake Pepin.

Likewise, Minnesota Department of Natural Resources fisheries crews found a mere seven species of fish in a stretch from St. Paul to Hastings that should have produced dozens. The reason was clear: Bacteria robbed the river of oxygen as it broke down

ABOVE: Great egrets stalk a Mississippi backwater south of La Crescent.

raw and partially treated sewage. Said Jack Enblom, DNR river surveys project supervisor, the biologists' gill net "was so filled with toilet paper and condoms they had to go home."

Now the good news: Improvements to the Pigs Eye sewage treatment plant and the Twin Cities' storm and sanitary sewer system have vastly reduced

so thick one summer night that Transportation Department plows cleared a foot of mayfly bodies from the Interstate 494 bridge in South St. Paul and sanded the roadway. During a recent fisheries survey, workers netted 25 walleyes and more than 170 saugers in a single lift. The fish stuck from the net "like quills from a porcupine," Enblom reported.

One recent spring, I walked the wooded hillsides of the Mississippi in the Katharine Ordway Natural History Study Area with David Clugston, then the resident naturalist. The private reserve, owned by Macalaster College, borders River Lake, one of many backwaters south of the Twin Cities. "Just this year I found a beaver lodge on the end of that peninsula and also some giant floater clams, which aren't supposed to be here because of the water quality," Clugston reported.

the sewage load and increased the dissolved oxygen in the Mississippi. Recently, Fremling found more than 400 *Hexagenia* mayfly nymphs in a square meter of river mud north of Hastings, where previously he had seen none. While he had recorded only eight mass emergences of mayflies during his earlier survey, he now logged 22 in a single summer. Mayflies flew

"Those are hopeful signs that the water quality is improving, but we have a long way to go." As he finished speaking, I looked up to see a bald eagle soar across River Lake and land in the upper branches of a tree by the river. Moments later, it was joined by another. All this less than ten miles from downtown St. Paul.

ABOVE: An egret spears a fish at Pigs Eye Lake.
RIGHT: Beautiful but destructive, nonnative purple loosestrife often dominates wetlands, such as this channel at the confluence of the Minnesota and Mississippi rivers.

ABOVE: Waterfowl navigate a side channel of the Mississippi near the Franklin Avenue Bridge in Minneapolis.

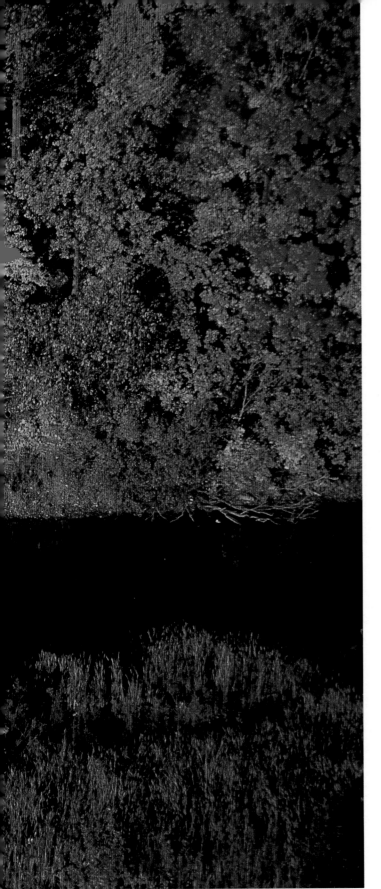

RED WING, WABASHA, WINONA. THE MISSISSIPPI
cuts deep against high limestone bluffs. River towns
nestle in the shadows of the hills, as though cupped
in the river's hand. These are some of the oldest
towns in Minnesota, built as shipping and settlers
ventured upriver.

The first boats to ply these waters were canoes.
Then came log and lumber rafts, keelboats and
flatboats. The first steamboat to reach Minnesota,
the *Virginia*, pulled into Fort Snelling in 1823.
Thereafter, steamboats churned up and down river,
with passengers and cargo. River trade was
threatened at the turn of the century by the
rapidly expanding network of railroads across the
nation's torso. But river traffic revived after the
1930s, when the U.S. Corps of Engineers completed
a system of locks and dams from the Twin Cities to
St. Louis to create a nine-foot-deep channel
capable of carrying towboats and barges.

The boats and barges that course the river seem
mammoth from water level. A friend and I sat in a
canoe one evening as a towboat churned upriver,
pushing a barge whose slanted prow plowed aside
frightful volumes of water as it loomed larger and
blacker and threatened to splatter us against the
riprapped shore. The pilot veered away, following
the deep-water channel rather than making flotsam
of a couple of fishermen. The barge and boat rushed
past 100 feet away, and then left us bobbing in a
wake that dashed the shore for five minutes.

Mississippi tributaries draining Minnesota and
Wisconsin lose speed as they hit the bottomlands of
the bigger river and drop their load of mud and
sand, forming deltas and backwaters. In fact, the
Chippewa River drops so much sand that it dams
the big river, forming Lake Pepin. The Corps'
system of dams inundated these backwaters, creating
a maze of channels. In the years that followed,
flights of ducks and gamefish filled these newly
flooded marshes. More recently, however, the

productivity of the backwaters has slackened because of sedimentation and the inevitable aging that seems to follow the creation of new reservoirs.

Still, the bottomlands are a fascinating maze, rich in beauty and life. On a canoe trip down the Cannon River, below the town of Welch, we suddenly discovered that our river was disappearing into a knot of braided channels. Time and again, we decided right or left, always choosing the channel that seemed to have the strongest current. For a long time we were lost in a secluded world of tall grass, cattails, and willows. Widely spaced dead trees stood above the delta. In several, bald eagles perched—as though they were beacons marking our way out (or buzzards waiting for our final, disastrous choice). Finally, we used our paddles to pole through a mucky channel so narrow that grass brushed the sides of our canoes. Suddenly we emerged in a channel of the Mississippi.

LEFT: The Mississippi valley spreads wide upstream from O.L. Kipp State Park.
ABOVE: An eastern redcedar clings to a hillside.

MY FRIEND TIM AND I SLIDE HIS JOHNBOAT INTO something called Goose Lake, a mere bay in a sprawling, shallow backwater called Weaver Bottoms. Flat-topped bluffs surround us in the hazy distance, the land folded on either shore in ridges and coulees like a rumpled blanket. The wind howls out of the south as Tim rows and I pepper the shore-line with a spinnerbait for northern pike. Rafts of diving ducks beat their wings against the waves to get airborne. More than a dozen white pelicans sail over the marsh, tilting their wings and disappear-ing behind bottomland forest. We slip into a side channel filled with cattails and willows. A low-flying marsh hawk flares and shows its distinctive white rump as it flies away. A flock of more than 30 cormorants passes overhead.

All that, but no fish. We don't see a pike that day until, as we are driving back to the Twin Cities along the Minne-sota side of the river, we decide to fish at the mouth of a creek that tumbles out of the limestone hills into Lake Pepin. We park the car and hike a couple hundred yards down the railroad track that runs tight against the west side of the Mississippi. Tim simply dangles a jig over the edge of the railroad bridge that crosses the little creek. Within seconds, he catches his pike, a fish of about three pounds.

We spend the late afternoon fishing from the bridge and the riprap that forms a steep slope between the tracks and the river. The low spring sun warms the hills. Every half-hour or so, a train bears down from St. Paul. You can hear the roar of the diesels far off round the bend. Then a high-pitched whine begins to build in the tracks as if they were banshees. I fear several tons of stressed steel will suddenly spring from the ties, killing us both. The whistle sounds, and the ballast begins to shake and rumble as we skip away from the track and take cover in the riprap boul-ders below the grade. As the freight train whistles by ten feet away, I huddle next to a chunk of lime-stone, with the strong river close at hand.

Only as the train passes do I lift my head and follow its course southward—downriver, toward Hannibal, St. Louis, Memphis, and New Orleans. That train is nothing compared to the river. Down here, the river has power. That much was proven with crush-ing authority during the floods of 1993. But the Mississippi also has symbolic power. Mingled in the river's dark waters is something more than the nation's topsoil and sewage and chemicals. Here, too, is America's life and history. As Mark Twain said, the river is a "wonderful book [with] a new story to tell every day." As I watch the train disap-pear down the long cradle of the blue river bluffs, I feel not like a fisherman, but like a character caught in the web of the river's plot.

ABOVE: Fall floodwaters surround a maple.
RIGHT: Minnehaha Creek spills over its landmark falls.

LEFT: A barred owl watches the bottomland forest.
ABOVE: Fallen leaves glide on the river.
BOTTOM: A gray squirrel gathers food.

Into the Bogs

Canoe Country

To the Lake

Wild Rivers

The North Shore

A Gathering
of Waters

Prairie Patchwork

Coulee Country

Wild
Rivers

A GOOD SHARE OF THE KETTLE RIVER WAS running up my nose and flowing through my sinuses. The rest of its powerful current swept me down the huge ledge of sandstone that forms the rapids known as Blueberry Slide. The silhouette of my kayak loomed overhead. Black shadows of boulders crowded around my shoulders. Except that rocks struck my helmet, it was a surprisingly peaceful world. I was impressed most of all by the amber light and rush of bubbles—like the apocalyptic tunnel of light that leads the dying to the afterlife. But I was afraid, because I could no longer breathe. I forced my paddle into position to do an Eskimo roll.

The river laughed and pushed me down again. That was it. I severed my fate from that of the kayak. In a word, I bailed, leaving the muffled, subdued world below the water and bursting into the noisy and confused world above. The rush of water and crash of waves filled my ears. Rocks bruised my rear end as I tumbled down the rapids. My friend Tom swung his kayak in front of me, and I grabbed the stern loop. Aided by my feeble, toad-like kicks, he pulled me into an eddy.

The Kettle River and I were just getting acquainted. Despite the rocky introduction, not all of our encounters have been so upsetting. Over the years, I have found in the Kettle and nearby St. Croix River, which receives the Kettle's bog-stained waters, two of my favorite streams. The Cloquet may be more remote, the North Shore streams more spectacular, the Mississippi more evocative of our nation's heritage, yet the Kettle and St. Croix are uniquely wild and beautiful.

The St. Croix was among the nation's first wild and scenic rivers, designated in 1968. It is still the only federal wild and scenic river in Minnesota. In 1975, the Kettle became the first stream in the *state's* wild and scenic rivers system. Both streams are protected in their natural condition by large public land holdings along their shores, including several state forests and parks. In fact, Minnesota's largest state park, St. Croix, lies at the rivers' confluence.

THE ST. CROIX HAS LONG been an important transportation route. It rises in northern Wisconsin, in the same stretch of boggy ground that feeds the Bois Brule River. While the Brule flows north into Lake Superior, the St. Croix flows south to the Mississippi. Ojibwa Indians and, later, European explorers and traders paddled up one river and down the other to bridge two continental watersheds. The shallow upper St. Croix proved tough going in low water. The sandstone rapids, reported explorer Lt. James Allen in 1832, "seem to be interminable . . . the fragments of which, broken and strewed in the channel, have cut up my men's feet and the bottoms of the [birchbark] canoes, horribly."

The same shallow headwaters inconvenienced loggers, who swarmed to the country in the 1840s and 1850s. Once the federal government secured

PREVIOUS PAGE: The St. Louis plunges through a jagged gorge in Jay Cooke State Park on its wild ride toward Lake Superior.
LEFT: Kettle River's swirling waters form a pothole next to Blueberry Slide.
ABOVE: Dark ledges form Dragon's Tooth rapid.

land and timber rights from Ojibwa tribes by treaty in 1837, loggers attacked the virgin pineries stretching between the St. Croix and Mississippi rivers, perhaps the most abundant stands of white pine in the nation. They built low rock levees and log-and-timber dams in the St. Croix's headwaters to raise the level sufficiently so they could carry logs through the shallows. Sawmills sprung up downstream, giving rise to Minnesota's earliest towns,

including Stillwater. In all, 133 sawmills operated on the river.

A boom constructed of logs and chains stretched the width of the river, trapping logs at the head of Lake St. Croix, about two miles north of Stillwater. Logs were sorted by marks stamped on their ends, which identified the nearly 2,000 camps at work in the watershed.

The volume of timber coursing down the St. Croix was tremendous—ten billion board feet in all.

Logs frequently jammed in a sharp bend in the St. Croix Dalles, plugging the entire channel. In 1886, loggers worked for six weeks to free a jam 100 feet deep and more than two miles long.

In 1901, a single raft of logs, stretching a quarter-mile long and comprising nine million board feet of timber, headed downstream from Stillwater to the Mississippi. Despite this volume, loggers and settlers insisted that the timber bonanza would last forever. "Centuries will hardly exhaust the pineries above us," thundered *Minnesota Pioneer* editor James Goodhue. He was wrong. The last log passed through the St. Croix Boom in 1914. The St. Croix's old-growth timber harvest had reached its end.

SCATTERED MATURE white pine still cover the banks near the St. Croix's confluence with the Kettle, and a sea of birch, aspen, and other hardwoods fills the gaps. A knot of islands splits the river into several secluded channels. My friend Layne and I beach our canoe to swim on the pure sand beach that forms at the downstream end of one island.

We put in several days earlier at Gordon Dam, the spillway where the fledgling St. Croix first transforms from still water to stream. Experiencing a river as you paddle downstream is like watching your child grow. We saw the St. Croix mature as it picked up waters from the Namekagon (still in

ABOVE: The St. Croix glides toward the one-time lumber center of Stillwater.
RIGHT: Early winter snow highlights the St. Croix near Arcola.

Wisconsin), Upper Tamarack, Yellow, Lower Tamarack (which we paddled up a mile for a better look), Clam, and Kettle. Along the way we saw bald eagles, white-tailed deer, ospreys, great blue herons, beavers, muskrats, turkey vultures, various dickey birds, and a couple of eastern hognose snakes—one of which we cornered and picked up, even as it hissed like a cobra.

Days on the river have settled into a comfortable routine. Up at 6:30 A.M. Coffee and a big

ABOVE: Eastern redcedar reaches toward the St. Croix.

breakfast. (My next book, *Thirty Days to Thinner Arteries*, will feature the St. Croix diet—fried spuds, sausage, jalapenos and boiled coffee.)

On the river by nine. Fishing. Set camp by 7:30. Dinner. More fishing. Bedtime at 10:30. Hardly ambitious, but it has a soothing rhythm.

As we paddle, we establish fleeting relationships with fellow river travelers. Our canoe is faster than most others, but Layne and I squander our advantage in fishing and other diversions. As we swim, we talk briefly with a man and woman we will see off and on for three days. They are early risers, on the river by 7:30, passing our camp as we eat breakfast. But they turn in early, so we pass their camp each evening.

One morning we paddle by a flotilla of six canoes. An hour later, they pass us as we fish. Later, we overtake them as they swim. Then they float by as Layne and I poke around a small tributary. In the evening, we pass them as we look for a campsite. We pitch our tent a mile below their camp that evening and hear them singing across the foggy river. In the morning, they pass us as we eat breakfast, but two hours later, we catch up with them. We chat each time we meet. They are a church group of high school seniors from Illinois. Layne and I drop back to fish and catch up only as they are loading their canoes to go home. We wave good-bye and head downstream alone, knowing we will never see them again.

Except for the trade of canoes and the scarcity of pine, I often feel I am seeing the same river Daniel G. Du Lhut proclaimed in 1680 "a very fine river." I feel that way less often on a river like the Mississippi, which is flanked by houses and farms. The St. Croix has remained wild. The reason is partly geology, partly design.

The fertile prairies and hardwood forests in much of the Mississippi watershed were plowed into productive cropland. But even after loggers had cleared the pine from the St. Croix basin, farming never really took root in the sand hills of northern Wisconsin and the bogs and clay of east-central Minnesota.

When thunderstorms sweep the watersheds, the Mississippi runs muddy with the topsoil of farms and the greasy sheen of city streets. The St. Croix rises clear in comparison. The proof of the St. Croix's water quality lies in the diversity of its aquatic life. Among all of Minnesota's big rivers, the St. Croix has the widest variety of clams—more than three dozen species, including two on the federal endangered species list, the Higgin's eye mussel and winged mapleleaf mussel. The latter is found nowhere in the world except along a ten-mile stretch of the St. Croix below Taylors Falls.

To safeguard the St. Croix's wild character, Congress designated the upper stream a federal wild and scenic river a quarter of a century ago. Four years later, the stretch below St. Croix Falls was added to the system. Aggressive land purchase by the National Park Service, and existing state parks and forests located on both sides of the river, should ensure that the St. Croix remains wild and scenic.

IF THE ST. CROIX HAS STATELY BEAUTY, THE KETTLE has a dark side. In the family of wild rivers in the St. Croix basin, the Kettle is the lawless younger brother, known largely for disaster and danger.

The Kettle made history in one of the most dramatic events of Minnesota's pioneer days. During the Hinkley Fire of 1894, residents of Sandstone fled to safety in the river as the ferocious forest fire swept the Kettle River valley, killing more than 400.

A couple of years later, the town of Banning was platted on the west bank of the Kettle, along the rapids that now carry the site's name. Some 300 people lived here. Many quarried sandstone from the cliffs. More than 20 million tons of rock were shipped by railroad during the years around the turn of the century. The town, however, lost out in competition to the quarries at nearby Sandstone. By the end of World War I, the railroad tracks were torn out, severing Banning's ties to the outside world. Today, massive concrete walls of the quarry's rock crusher and power house stand incongruously amid birch and pine. Saplings grow from stagnant pools inside the powerhouse, rising above the roofless walls. It seems a decrepit and joyless Japanese garden. The thunder of mining equipment and steam engines is gone. What remains is the constant voice of the nearby Kettle, running its rocky course to the St. Croix.

To people today, the Kettle's rapids make the river memorable. The season for running white water begins in April, when the bogs in the Kettle's headwaters spring free from winter and the snow disappears from the bluffs. Add a hard spring rain, and the river fills the channel to the banks. The Banning Rapids roar with power. Still, novices underestimate the river's force. Without experienced companions to guide them, they fail to recognize the dangers in the explosive standing waves and undercut cliffs that characterize this stretch of water, and they paddle blithely to their death.

ABOVE: High spring water reflects the bottomland forest near Marine on St. Croix.
RIGHT: Ferns grow from the Kettle's sandstone cliffs in Banning State Park.

Even with practice and many successful runs behind me, I need time to work off the jitters. We gather in the boat landing above the rapids. I feel as if I've had too much coffee, so I try a few handstands and calisthenics to stretch my muscles. I fasten the chin strap on my helmet and make sure my life vest is secure. I slide into the boat, settle into the cockpit, and snap the spray skirt into place. I push off into the river, lean from side to side as I brace on my paddle, take a few strong strokes upstream to warm up, then set myself loose on the current.

The slick surface of the Kettle begins to ripple and break as I look down the long slope of water called Blueberry Slide. (The slide is obvious; the blueberries on the banks won't be in evidence until July.) At the bottom of the drop, the Kettle rears up into a three-foot standing wave. I've been down this way many times since my first season on the Kettle, but I still feel the lightning rush of adrenaline. I gauge my swift route down the rippling sandstone ledge, draw hard a few strokes at the last moment, and crash into the standing wave. Spray hits my face. I lean into the wave and plant my paddle in the solid water behind the crest. As I pull toward an eddy to rest, I feel as though I've crossed the threshold to another world—the world of the river. My ears are filled with the white noise of the river talking.

The rest of the day we play in the canyon, surfing our kayaks on the standing waves and racing from eddy to eddy down the gorge. Spring sunlight sparkles off the river's jewels. We almost forget to look for the gloomy walls of the old quarry buildings

LEFT: The Kettle races through Mother's Delight rapids in Banning State Park.

as we race by. They are of a different world. We enter a shadowy stretch of river, where the Kettle glides quietly between sandstone cliffs. On the right, a pothole, or "kettle," was cut thousands of years ago by glacial floodwaters, which swirled pebbles in a depression in the soft sandstone. Since then, the river has dropped, exposing the pothole and its breached side wall to form a cave. I paddle in and look up, as if I were staring up a chimney. I watch a pine tree above, framed by rock, as my kayak twirls in the eddy.

Finally, we tackle the last rapids of the day. The smooth river gathers up again and gains speed down a broken stretch of waves and boulders. Ahead, two sandstone cliffs pinch the river down to a narrow passage. This rapids is the best-known of all, perhaps because it has the most sinister name: Hell's Gate. Beyond lies flat water and the town of Sandstone—the end of the magical river world. And so I wonder as my boat dances down the breaking waves through these gates of sandstone, "Is this rapids named for where I've been? That couldn't be. It must be named for where I'm going."

Sure enough, it's true. After bounding through the rapids, we soon hit slack water, and a hellish strong wind blows upstream.

RIGHT: Harebells find a foothold in sandstone cliffs overhanging the Kettle.

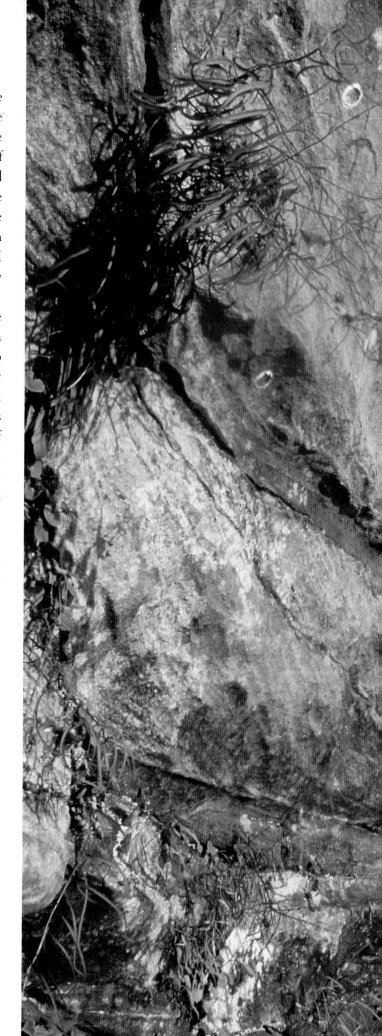

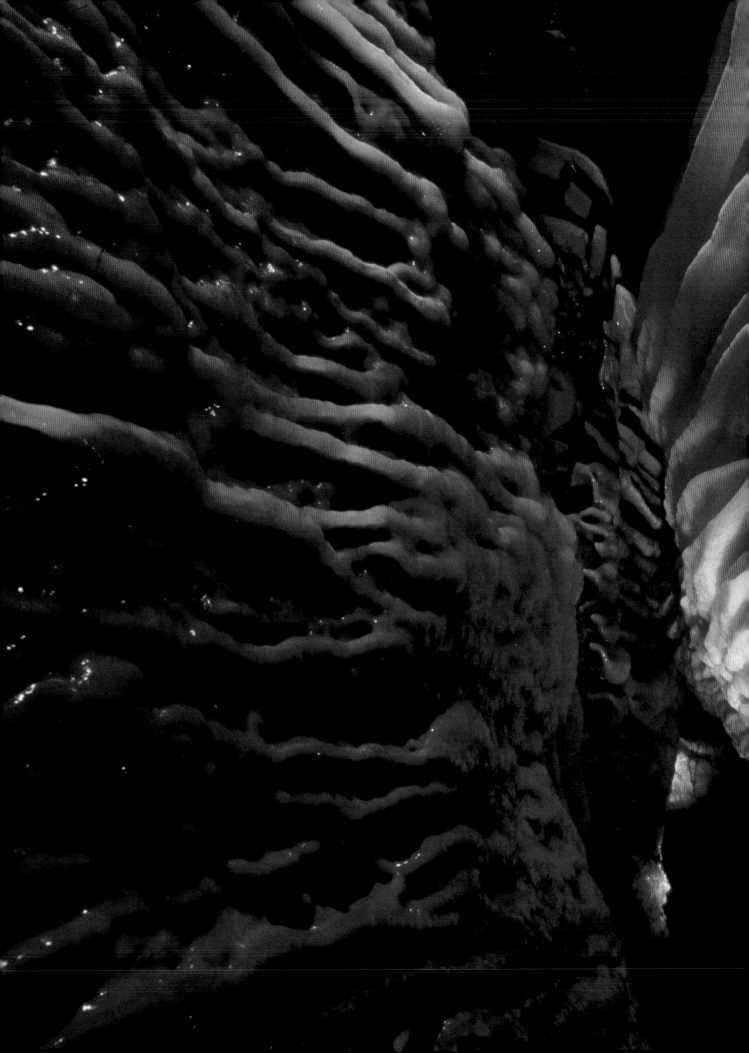

Into the Bogs

Canoe Country

To the Lake

Wild Rivers

The North Shore

A Gathering of Waters

Prairie Patchwork

Coulee Country

Coulee Country

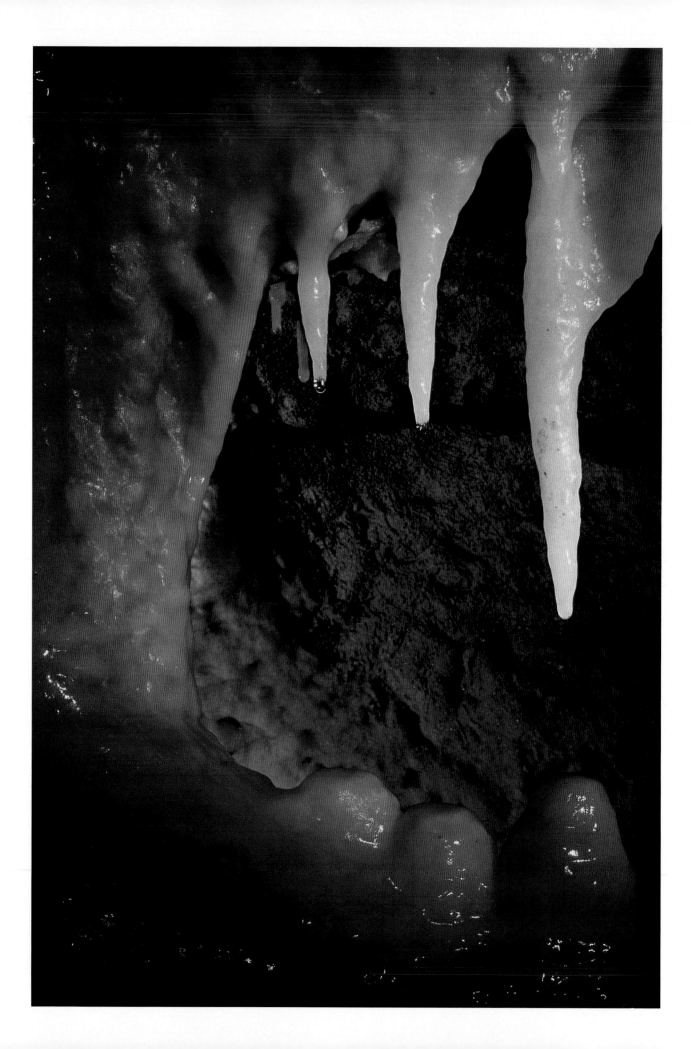

CLOSE YOUR EYES—TIGHT. KEEP THEM CLOSED until all images are gone, and the only thing that remains is black, just a solid matrix of black, the blackest black you can imagine. Now open your eyes: The black remains. You can feel your eyelids move—one moment closed, another open. But the black stays always the same.

That's what it's like to be in Mystery Cave when you've bumped your flashlight and it has gone out. There I stand, feet jammed heel to toe in a deep crevice, where my helmet likewise is wedged so that I can look only over my right shoulder. By pressing my back against the rock behind me, I can take weight off my feet long enough to inch them to the right. I press, shuffle my feet, and settle in again. Six inches of progress.

Finally, I see a flashlight beam to my right. "How much farther?" I call out.

"You're about halfway through," Bill Morrissey says. Morrissey, director of parks for the Minnesota Department of Natural Resources, has become an enthusiastic spelunker since the state added the cave to Forestville State Park in 1988.

My arms tire, my weight sags, and my feet wedge tighter in the crevice. Panic sets in. I imagine the tons of rock around me shifting ever so slightly, an infinitesimal sigh in the body of the earth, and suddenly I am lodged between two immovable slabs of the planet, while a few dozen yards above me sparrows sprint on the wind.

"How far now?"

"You're two-thirds, three-quarters of the way. You're almost done."

By the time I emerge from the other end of the crack, I know I will be a long time in becoming a caver. And I have a new perspective on southeastern Minnesota, a topsy-turvy country where hills are plains, valleys are hills, and solid ground is run through with empty space and subterranean streams.

I first really noticed this country nearly 20 years ago, when I was working a river survey for the DNR. Rain had been falling for hours. We sped down the Root River on high, muddy water. As we drifted east toward Lanesboro, slipping deeper into the river valley, limestone bluffs rose high on either side. As sun finally broke through the clouds, the bottomlands sighed a muggy breath that carried turkey vultures above the hilltops. Flanked on either side by cliffs and a jungle of hardwood forest, I felt as though the Root had carried us far beyond the borders of Minnesota.

Truth is, there's much that sets the southeast apart from the rest of the state—its geology, its landscape, and even its plants and wildlife. Why? A good place to find the answer is in the darkest dark of Mystery Cave.

Located about 30 miles southeast of Rochester, Mystery Cave was discovered in February 1937,

PREVIOUS PAGE: Looking up, limestone formations guard the entrance to Garden of the Gods in Mystery Cave.
LEFT: Dissolved calcium forms stalactites in Mystery Cave.
ABOVE: These distinctive stalactites have been dubbed Carrot Sticks.

when a local named Joe Petty was hiking down the banks of the South Branch of the Root River and noticed steam rising from the riverbank. Poking into the rocks, he found what proved to be an opening to one of the main sections of the cave. Since then, more than 12 miles of cave have been explored and mapped, ranking it as the nation's 32nd-longest cavern.

The cave walls, like much of southeastern Minnesota's bedrock, are limestone and dolomite, made up of the calcareous remains of shellfish that lived in the seas covering most of North America several hundred million years ago. Since the land uplifted and seas drained away, groundwater seeping

ABOVE: Eroding limestone forms Coyote Bluff in Whitewater State Park.

and a half underground as the Disappearing River before it rejoins the main stem of the stream at an area called Seven Springs.

In fact, much of southeastern Minnesota's hill country is undermined by fissures, some perhaps more spectacular than Mystery Cave but still unknown. Driving through the area in winter, Morrissey pointed out dark, tree-fringed depressions in the snowy fields. "Farmers didn't leave those trees there because they like nature," he remarked. Indeed, the untillable areas are sinkholes, shallow-lying caverns of various sizes that have undermined the surface. Occasionally, they give way beneath a tractor or even gobble up a house.

Geology contributes, naturally, to the above-ground appearance of the land as well. If you look at a map of Minnesota, you can see that the lakes dotting the central and south-central parts of the state abruptly end at a line defined roughly by Interstate 35 south from the Twin Cities. There's a reason for that—the same reason that the southeast is laced with hills and carved by deep river valleys.

The ice sheet that covered most of Minnesota as recently as 10,000 to 12,000 years ago never visited southeastern Minnesota (though far older glaciers covered even the southeast). So, as glaciers rejuvenated the face of the land, forming the low hills and shallow depressions that would become the Land of 10,000 Lakes, streams in the southeast continued to carve the deep wrinkles of old age.

What is left is not hill country so much as it is valley country—or coulee country, as they call it down here. Where you seem to be driving up into hills, as though into the foothills of mountains, you're actually heading out of a valley. If you're hiking along a creek bottom and decide to climb the nearest hill for a look around, you may be surprised. Expecting to reach a summit, you may battle your way up a slope through thicket and woods, only to find a flat plain planted in corn.

through the bedrock has dissolved calcite in the rock, opening fissures and caverns. In the case of Mystery Cave, glacial meltwater drained through the cavern at various periods during the last 160,000 years, excavating broad passageways. Even today, part of the South Branch of the Root River slips into the bowels of the cave and flows a mile

THE LIMESTONE GEOLOGY GIVES BIRTH TO ANOTHER feature that distinguishes the southeast from the rest of Minnesota—its many trout streams. Abundant springs and seepages provide a steady supply of the cold water needed by trout. After its detour through Mystery Cave, the South Branch of the Root becomes one of the state's best trout streams. Nearby Canfield and Forestville creeks, tiny streams that harbor hundreds of trout per mile, spring

directly from hillside caverns. Dissolved calcium from the limestone fosters a proliferation of the aquatic insects eaten by trout.

The limestone geology has also protected rare plants, remnants of the ice age, thousands of years after these species disappeared from the rest of Minnesota. Icy winter air flowing into subterranean fissures freezes pockets of groundwater. The ice, which remains frozen through summer, cools air flowing through the fissures, creating an air-conditioned environment where the passages emerge at the foot of a cliff. In these micro-climates live rare plants closely related to arctic plants, such as Iowa golden saxifrage. Tiny snails, thought to have been extinct since the ice age, have recently been discovered. Apparently, these cold-weather species were stranded in their ice-age niches as glaciers retreated and temperate weather prevailed all around.

In the wooded valleys of Rice and Goodhue counties grows a rare and unique flower found nowhere else in the world—the dwarf trout lily. The plant apparently evolved from the similar white trout lily. Yet one must have doubts about the dwarf trout lily's future. Its only known pollinator, the minor bee, prefers the flower's much more common relative. And the dwarf trout lily produces seeds rarely if at all, instead sprouting from runner bulbs at a rate barely high enough to maintain its numbers. Diminutive and frail, extremely limited in geographic range, the dwarf trout lily invites the question: What is a species worth, especially one that seems to have adapted itself into an evolutionary corner? The stock answer is that we must protect the diversity of life, that we don't know how valuable a species such as the dwarf trout lily might prove to be. I'm sympathetic to the protection of rare species. I believe that extinction provides a warning of the much more critical loss of habitat

ABOVE: Recently introduced to Minnesota, wild turkeys proliferate in coulee country.
RIGHT: Marsh marigolds dot the forest floor in spring.

that eventually threatens entire communities of plants and animals and weakens the web of life. Yet the dwarf trout lily—like millions of species before it—seems destined to fall into the chasm of extinction. It pains me to say so, but I can't understand why I would mourn its passing.

On a larger scale, the southeast is warmer than the forests to the north; wetter than the prairies to the west. For that reason, the forest resembles the woods of the southern Midwest and the Ozarks, with a preponderance of oaks and species such as shagbark hickory, black walnut, butternut, witch hazel, and Kentucky coffee tree. The undergrowth is junglelike, filled with grapevines and stinging nettle.

The Karner blue butterfly, recently added to the federal endangered species list, lives nowhere in Minnesota except the sandy ravines and oak savannas of Whitewater Wildlife Management Area. More wild turkeys live in the southeast than in any other part of the state. The region is also the only part of Minnesota that harbors bobwhite quail, which can't survive harsh winters. Driving the back roads at night, you stand a good chance of seeing (or flattening) a possum. High on the rocky bluffs live timber rattlesnakes; in the backwaters of the Mississippi lives the smaller and much rarer massasauga. Neither rattlesnake is found anywhere else in Minnesota.

EARLY SETTLERS EXTERMINATED RATTLESNAKES by finding their wintering dens and destroying the reptiles by the hundreds. The settlers were hard on this country in other ways as well.

Because steamboats offered easy passage up the Mississippi River, coulee country became the first part of Minnesota to be settled by whites. Towns began appearing in the 1840s. After the 1851 Mendota treaty wrested control of the area from the Dakota Indians, steamers and then railroads brought a flood of settlers.

Wheat farms dotted the upland prairies and the river valleys and terraces. Settlers logged, grazed, and plowed the hillsides. Stripping native vegetation from the steep slopes triggered tremendous erosion and unleashed spectacular floods. For decades, silt washed out of the hills, muddying streams and covering farms and communities in the valleys below. In 1938 the town of Beaver, nestled in the valley of Beaver Creek, flooded 28 times. Today, the townsite lies buried in sediment.

Salvation finally came to the region in the form of Richard J. Dorer, a game manager with the state Department of Conservation and a tireless proselytizer for conservation causes. Dorer rallied support for improving farming practices, restoring natural vegetation to erodible hillsides, saving wetlands, and protecting sensitive and valuable wildlife areas through public ownership. He even wrote poetry

ABOVE: White trout lilies grow in southeastern woodlands.
RIGHT: Once the beds of ancient seas, limestone underlies the southeast.

about Minnesota's resources. When Dorer died in 1973, he was buried in a cemetery overlooking Beaver, but his memory lives on in the naming of Richard J. Dorer Memorial Hardwood Forest, a far-flung collection of public lands in southeastern Minnesota that includes some of the most scenic hill country and hardwood forests in the state.

Despite conservation efforts, the problems of flooding, erosion, and siltation persist. Valley towns still flood after hard rains. Rivers such as the Cannon, Zumbro, and Root are quick to muddy up as runoff strips topsoil from farmland. The downstream reaches of all major streams are layered in sand. Recently, a friend and I fished for trout in the lower section of Hay Creek, just a couple miles above Red Wing. Lew waded upstream, I headed down. After half an hour, I went to find him.

I soon heard him holler: "Greg, I'm stuck."

When I finally spotted him, he was mired to his thighs in the sandy streambed, water lapping at the tops of his waders. I slid a long, dead branch out to him, and he climbed hand over hand to the bank.

THERE ARE MILES OF BEAUTIFUL BACK ROADS HERE. They soar over ridges and plunge down the valleys. I'm always amazed when I'm driving along the cultivated uplands and I suddenly drop into a creek valley, hardwood forest and bluffs closing in on both sides. On I drive, until the creek joins a river and the valley opens up as if the land itself is being pried apart.

Place names here ring with strangeness: Rattlesnake Ridge, Hoosier Ridge, German Ridge, Sleepy Valley, Whiskey Hill, Funk Ford, Boston Coulee. The twisting topography is tough to follow on a map; tougher still in three dimensions.

The river towns down here are tight-knit, with a real beauty of composition. This is partly due to their age and the richness of the old brick and limestone block from which they're built. But mainly it is a matter of topography. Framed by hills, they address a river—whether the town is as large as Red Wing or as small as Elba. I think I have never seen a community more beautiful than Lanesboro on the day after my wedding, when my wife and I dropped into the valley of the South Branch of the Root in a peaceful snow and saw the old buildings and the soft street lights blanketed in white.

LEFT AND RIGHT: Centerpiece of Whitewater State Park, the Whitewater River is a premier trout stream.
OVERLEAF: Canada geese burst through sunlight over a coulee near Winona.

Still, a car window provides a sterile view of country. To get to know it, hike a path or paddle a stream so you can feel the mass of the land beneath your feet, or the power of a river against the paddle in your hand. Whitewater, Forestville, Beaver Creek Valley, and Carley state parks offer trails that wind from shaded bottomland to wide-open bluff top. Less well known are state forest parcels, which include trails for hiking, snowmobiling, skiing, and

horseback riding. The 27,500-acre Whitewater Wildlife Management Area offers plenty of room to roam. The paved Root River State Trail carries bicyclists through river bottoms and bluff lands between Fountain and Rushford. The Cannon Valley Trail winds from Cannon Falls to Red Wing.

One of the most pleasant ways to penetrate the back country of southeastern Minnesota is by river. Three streams (in addition to the Mississippi) are large enough to consistently float a canoe: the Cannon, Zumbro and Root. The Cannon,

northernmost of the three, least typifies the area. Its upper reaches lie on gently rolling, glaciated land. Only as it leaves Byllesby Reservoir near Cannon Falls does the riffling current cut deep into the limestone bedrock. The Zumbro and Root, however, flow through deep gorges, where shadows cast magic on quick, easy rapids and still pools.

Yet nowhere does the stunning interplay of water, rock, and life converge so clearly as in the matrix of a trout stream. Even if you're not a fisherman, probe the riffles—overturning rocks to look for the abundant mayfly, stonefly, and caddis fly nymphs that form the foundation of the stream's hierarchy of life. Or silently slip along the bank to watch brown trout sip insects drifting on the water's surface. There's much to learn about fishing—and nature—by simply watching. And if you're lucky you may witness a "hatch," the magical moment when nymphs of mayflies or other aquatic insects respond to unknown signals and simultaneously swim to the surface and split their nymphal shucks to emerge as winged adults. By the thousands or even millions, they escape the bounds of their watery habitat, like champagne bubbles rising and bursting at the surface. The trout respond to this bonanza, feasting ever more ravenously and carelessly on the insects that linger on the water. The fossiliferous limestone of the streambed, which captured and preserved the remains of life millions of years ago, seems now to set it free.

ABOVE: A female cardinal takes a respite from winter feeding.
RIGHT: Once covering millions of acres, oak savanna now exists only as remnants such as this in Katharine Ordway Natural History Study Area.

Into the Bogs

Canoe Country

To the Lake

Wild Rivers

The North Shore

A Gathering
of Waters

Prairie Patchwork

Coulee Country

Prairie
Patchwork

I N SOUTHWESTERN MINNESOTA, A RIDGE OF SIOUX quartzite erupts from the landscape like a surgery scar. Its appearance in the hazy distance gives rise to the name Blue Mounds—now the name of the state park where it is found. But up close, it's neither blue nor mound-shaped. It's an abrupt cliff, up to 90 feet high and more than a mile long, looking as though the flat prairie landscape has momentarily lost its vertical hold—one plane of earth sitting inexplicably 90 feet above the other. The cliff face is deeply incised and jagged, the rock purplish like a bruise. Maybe God began making the earth at this spot, proceeded off toward the southeast, and when he had worked his way around the globe, found he was a bit off and decided, "Good enough, no one will notice here anyway." And he just left it, as I might leave a mismatched seam of wallpaper in the corner behind the curtains.

I'm standing on the edge, looking off in the great distance, farther than any living person can see. I spot a vast herd of tens of thousands of bison. They move in a great brown wave. There are no individuals, just the herd moving as a single organism, sliding like a rippling pelt of buffalo hide through the tallgrass toward the horizon. Off they run—off to Buffalo Ridge and north to Buffalo River.

I am imagining this, of course. Bison haven't roamed freely in Minnesota since 1880. In reality, I see the town of Luverne about four miles away. A speeding truck kicks up a roostertail of dust. A checkerboard of crops and farms stretches into the distance. If the day were clear, without this humid haze, I could see perhaps 25 miles in most directions—a sweep of vision encompassing as much as 2,000 square miles. And almost all of it—except this patch of prairie I'm standing on and the pockets of cottonwoods in the creek bottoms off in the distance—is artificial. We don't often think of it, but just about everything about farmland—the verdant, bucolic scene of many of our ancestors—is unnatural: the corn and beans, bare dirt, Eurasian weeds, and planted windbreaks.

Yet as I step back and follow the hiking trail away from the cliff, I can indulge myself in an illusion. Dipping down into a swale, I'm suddenly surrounded by prairie clear out to my limited horizons, and a clear blue vault of prairie sky overhead. Indian grass and big bluestem bend and flatten in the wind, their color changing as they sway this way and that, creating the illusion that the grass runs like the bison. Wrote Sherwood Anderson: "Mystery whispered in the grass." And John Madson: "The open land was calculated to turn a man in on himself. A land without echoes or shadow except the one cast by him."

Fortunately, such places without echoes and shadows still remain. Several dozen high-quality prairie sites—such as Blue Mounds State Park—are protected as parks, wildlife management areas, state scientific and natural areas, or preserves owned by a nonprofit group called The Nature Conservancy. Within these tiny remnants, it's possible to step into

PREVIOUS PAGE: Fluffy as a cloud, prairie smoke covers a prairie near Wadena.
LEFT: Blazing star enlivens the Bicentennial Prairie near Felton.
ABOVE: By their appearance at a distance, Sioux quartzite cliffs give rise to the name Blue Mounds.

the tallgrass prairie and oak savanna that once swept in a great crescent down the Red River Valley and across southwestern, southern, and southeastern Minnesota.

Minnesota's prairies were once part of a spectrum of grasslands that stretched from the front range of the Rockies eastward to Ohio. The driest and sparsest of these, called the shortgrass plains, lay in the rain shadow of the mountains in what is now eastern Montana, Wyoming, and Colorado. Across the Dakotas, Nebraska, and Kansas, slightly greater rainfall and lusher, taller plants characterized the mixed-grass prairie. Farther east, including Minnesota, grew the tallgrass prairie, named for the dominant big bluestem and Indian grasses, which grow taller than a man. Also in this wetter eastern region grew oak savanna, a beautiful landscape of scattered oak and oak groves with an open understory that resembled shaggy parkland. The former extent of this tallgrass prairie coincides neatly with today's Corn Belt—same rainfall, different crop.

While climate provided the conditions that created prairie, constant wildfires maintained the prairie. Some fires were sparked by lightning. Some were set by Indians to drive game or provide better grazing. The blazes would roar and crackle across tens of thousands of acres at a time. Fires rejuvenated prairie plants by removing dead plant material and quickly returning nutrients to the soil. Fires also drove back the cottonwoods that crept out of the draws and the aggressive young oaks that would otherwise march outward from the perimeters of prairie groves.

The combination of desiccating weather and frequent fires favored the evolution and growth of perennial plants with deep root systems. Not only did the plant reach deep for water, but most of it was protected from the fire that licked the surface of the earth. The dotted blazing star, which grows

ABOVE: Growing taller than a person, big bluestem is a dominant part of the tallgrass prairie.
OVERLEAF: The setting sun pierces cloudy prairie sky in Hubbard County.

about two feet tall, sends out a system of roots nine feet across and 16 feet deep.

Frequent grazing by animals such as bison favored the dominance of grasses. Grasses grow from the stem base rather than the tips, so if a blade of grass is chewed down, the stem continues to send up a shoot. If the grass is grazed down to the base, it forms the clump of grass characteristic of prairie turf.

flower, leadplant, golden alexander, bush clover, prairie rose, blazing star, wild quinine, rattlesnake master, hoary puccoon, porcupine grass, dropseed grass, and more.

Such a dense matrix of deep-rooted plants did not submit easily to the plow. Roots snapped and popped like a constant barrage of fire at a carnival shooting gallery. The moist soil stuck to the plow like paste. But submit it did, as settlers streamed to the prairies of the new state of Minnesota. In 1878, the *Marshall Messenger reported*, "You can travel north, south, east, west, and everywhere you go, breaking teams are hard at work turning our rich soil."

As the prairie was settled, bison were killed and driven westward. Elk, grizzly bears, wolves, and mountain lions, too, had all but vanished by the late 1800s.

The multifarious native plants were also disappearing as prairie was planted in crops. Even non-arable land was heav-

And so the forces of fire, grazing, drought, and pollinating insects created a diverse mosaic in the prairie sod, including up to 300 species of flowering plants. Just recently, I was roaming a remnant of virgin prairie with a representative of The Nature Conservancy who mentioned that a single square meter of good prairie should contain at least 25 species, nearly all of them long-lived perennials. Then, looking in a small circle at his feet, he began pointing them out: downy phlox, prairie cone-

ily grazed and invaded by Eurasian weeds brought over by settlers. Soon, prairie was driven to the far corners of the country: stony hills and bluffs, the margins of pioneer cemeteries, and the right-of-ways of railroads, where cinders from locomotives and sparks from the wheels ignited the frequent fires that groomed these linear prairies. According to estimates, less than two percent of the state's prairies survive with a modest assemblage of tall-grass species.

ABOVE: A red admiral butterfly alights on a purple coneflower.
RIGHT: Goldenrod waves across Hole-in-the-Mountain Prairie, near Lake Benton.

Many of these prairie remnants have been purchased and protected by government or The Nature Conservancy. Yet protection isn't accomplished with the signing of the deed; land managers must restore the fire that maintained the prairies and battle the Eurasian weeds that compete with native plants for control of the prairie sod. Professional land managers, aided by enthusiastic volunteers, set prairies afire, clear brush, girdle encroaching trees to kill them, rip out exotic weeds, and gather seeds of native plants to use in restoring new areas. The result has been a small but flourishing patchwork of prairie across western and southern Minnesota. Most of these state, federal, and Conservancy prairies are open to the public.

Blue Mounds State Park is a case in point. Though once privately owned, prairie endured because the thin soil lying on the high side of the cliff was too rocky to plow. Nonetheless, heavy

ABOVE: A whitetail deer feeds among corn and oaks.
RIGHT: Gnarled oaks grow in the shelter of the Blue Mounds cliff.

grazing weakened and tore the fabric of native plants and provided an opening for weeds such as timothy and various thistles.

The first public land was purchased as a make-work project during the Depression. Prairie was hardly at issue. Works Progress Administration crews built two dams on Mound Creek to create two ponds. Subsequently, the state planted thousands of trees around the ponds and built a campground.

Not until much more recently did park managers take steps to restore prairie. Through controlled burning and weed control, they have encouraged the growth of native plants. Prickly-pear cactuses grow on rocky sites. Several rare plants grow by the vernal pools created as seepage and rainfall collect in shallow depressions of Sioux quartzite. During the growing season, a parade of colors marches across Blue Mounds as various grasses and wildflowers come into bloom.

And bison are back. A herd of about 65 grazes in a 120-acre fenced enclosure. Compared with the thousands that once rumbled across the wide-open plains, the Blue Mounds herd is a relic, a pitiful museum piece. Yet they hint at the glorious past. And sadly, this is the only way we have been able to preserve both the prairie and the most magnificent beast to roam it in modern times—as tiny, isolated patches woven into the greater fabric of our modern pattern of land use.

Even when taken piecemeal, prairie is a powerful landscape. The sky and space are overwhelming—and often ominous. Standing on a high knoll, I have watched thunderstorms rip across the plains in the distance. A friend of mine, caught in the open, lost nearly every window in his Jeep to a prairie hailstorm. Total bill to replace glass and sheet metal: more than $6,000.

Prairie often speaks with a different power. Not far from Blue Mounds are the Jeffers Petroglyphs, images hammered into a flat Sioux quartzite outcrop thousands of years ago. Today, the images are barely visible. Getting down on my knees, I match the cracks in the outcrop with the photos in my guidebook. Running my hand over the rock, I feel the glyphs. Only then do I begin to see them. With my finger, I trace out the atlatls and spears used by bison hunters before the advent of the bow and arrow. I look for bisons, thunderbirds, and shamans. I'm reminded that the prairie, like these petroglyphs, speaks sometimes as forcefully as a windstorm and at other times as softly as a breeze.

LEFT: Rainwater pools up on granite outcrops near Big Stone Lake.
ABOVE: Prairie grass peeks through windblown snow.

ABOVE: Wildfires groomed the low-lying plants beneath fire-resistant oaks in southern Minnesota.
RIGHT, TOP: Blazing star spreads across Prairie Coteau Scientific and Natural Area near Pipestone.
RIGHT, BOTTOM: Male prairie chicken puts on its courting display.

Into the Bogs

Canoe Country

The North Shore

To the Lake

Wild Rivers

A Gathering
of Waters

Prairie Patchwork

Coulee Country

To the
Lake

I'D BE A BIG-LEAGUE BALLPLAYER TODAY, MAYBE neck-and-neck with Dave Winfield for total base hits, except that nearly every weekend—when all the Little League games were scheduled—Dad, Mom, my kid brother and I piled into the car and headed for the lake. As we snaked along the two-lane blacktop around Mille Lacs Lake, Mom unpacked dinner—egg salad sandwiches and lemonade—which kept us going till nightfall, when our headlights knifed into the dark forest around Eagle Lake. On its shore sat the cabin that served as base camp for many of my childhood adventures.

Dad bought three acres during the war, when only two or three cabins sat on the shore. In 1956, he and my mom and uncle and aunt built the cabin, square as a brick of cheese with a big fireplace of field stone. While they worked, I caught frogs in the bulrushes by the lake and saved them in a big metal pail.

Up the lake a few hundred yards lived Joe Kolarik, who said he had played for the Pittsburgh Pirates in 1907. He'd tell me of coming to this region just north of the Whitefish Chain back when blacktop didn't run very far. He and a friend would drag a leaky wooden boat back into some mosquito hell to a lake no one fished. I imagine him now wearing a wool shirt, twill pants, and a brown felt fedora. He'd be casting a red and white wooden Bass-Oreno with a tubular steel fishing rod and machined brass bait-casting reel. "Back in those days," he would say, in a reedy, codgerly drawl, "the bass were so big they were ugly."

When I was 10, a copy of *Sports Afield* fell into my hands. Back then, outdoor writers still had literary aspirations. Their articles painted pictures and told stories. I think for that reason I got the bass-fishing bug in a big way. "It's six o'clock," Dad would say at my bedside, and while my mom and brother slept, we'd slip on our clothes, fetch a couple of cookies out of the breadbox and carry our tackle down to the boat.

Those first few minutes on the water were magic. Fog lay softly on the lake. A great blue heron stalked the shore. Dad rowed the boat. The brass gears of our reels whirred with every cast, as our big plugs sailed repeatedly in tall arcs toward the shallows. For the moment the lake was ours. But after a half-hour, the sun hit the water, an outboard started up somewhere else on the lake, and the magic evaporated like the fog.

The fishing was often good, occasionally memorable, but other incidents stick in my mind. Once as we cast along the shoreline, a great horned owl swooped down from a tree to try to snatch Dad's Jitterbug from the surface. Only by reeling fast and jerking the lure away did he avoid catching an owl. Several times more the owl dove from its perch to snatch at a plug, persisting until we had moved well down the shore.

Another day we motored across the water when the fog lay as thick as cotton. We could see no more

PREVIOUS PAGE: Sun sets on Blue Lake, north of Park Rapids.
LEFT: Waves wash the beach at Father Hennepin State Park, on Mille Lacs Lake.
ABOVE: A great blue heron stalks a wetland.

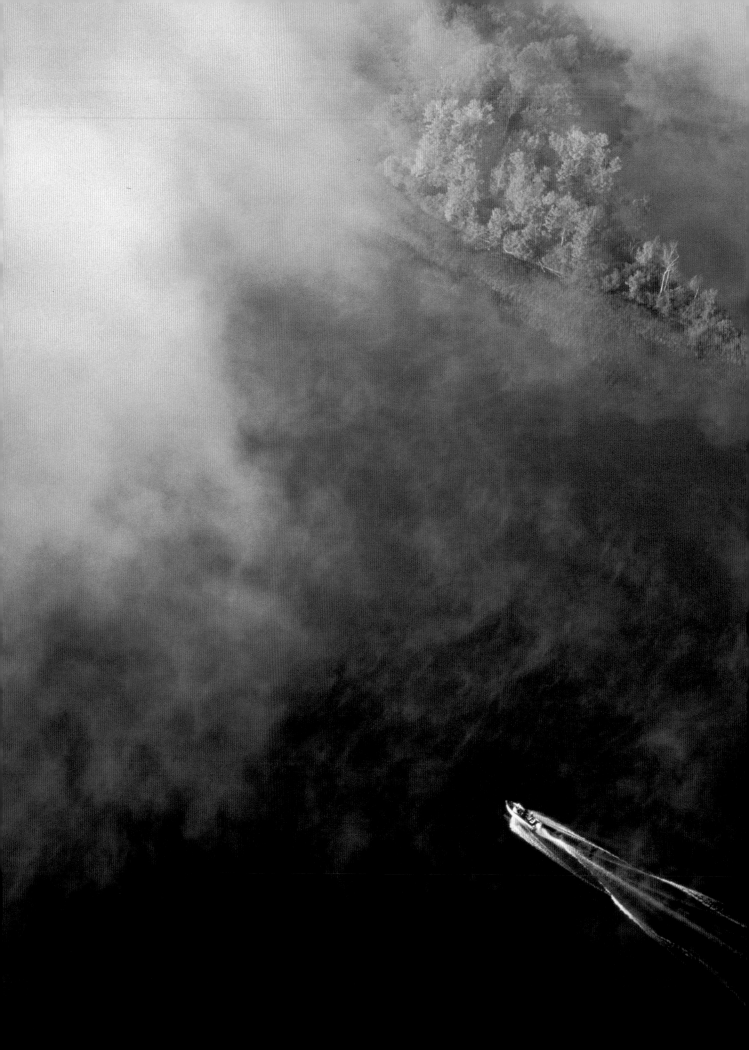

than a few boat lengths, though with a three-horse outboard, it's tough to imagine colliding hard enough with anything to do serious damage. Suddenly we burst upon a gathering of a dozen loons—lined up, yodeling, and prancing on the water as if they were at a barn dance.

Of course, that was then; this is now. These days, my wife and I plan our departure to miss the Friday afternoon traffic, which squeezes down the main highways out of town like a pig down a python. We are surrounded by a moveable car lot—autos, vans, pickups, and jeeps, stuffed with whiny kids and desperate parents. They pull boats and trailers, carry canoes and sailboards. Roadsides throughout lake country are posted with real estate signs. The lakes erupt with the sound of speedboats and jet-skis.

The sentimental carping of a middle-aged guy? Well, carping based on fact. Unquestionably, we're putting ever more pressure on our lakes—more people, more cabins, more boats, more pollution from lawn runoff and septic systems, more destruction of the shoreline vegetation needed by a variety of living creatures from fish to loons. And this is true in any of the state's popular lake and resort areas—from Brainerd to Detroit Lakes to Bemidji.

But you can still find solitude and wild country if you look. That is what I try to remember when I imagine that I sound like old Joe Kolarik.

One evening a couple of years ago, for example,

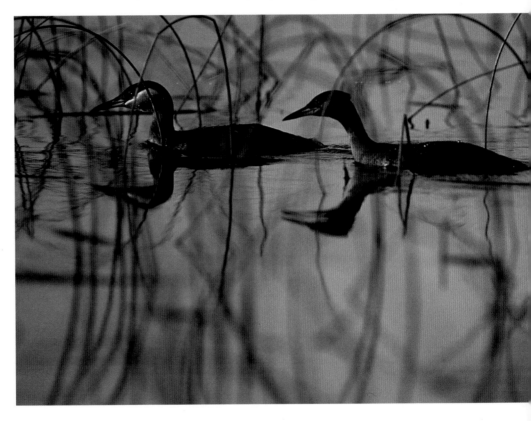

I was looking for a shortcut to the cabin from a lake called Wabedo in southern Cass County. Soon the blacktop petered out, and I was left looking down a lonely stretch of two-rut dirt road headed south across ten miles of some of the emptiest country around. It was dark, and I didn't know the way and I didn't know if the road went through, but it looked firm and fairly dry, so I pushed on. By the time I came out on the main highway, I had spotted nearly two dozen deer in my headlights. I later heard from the Cass County land commissioner that his foresters were seeing timber wolves in the area once again.

Just a few years ago, I decided to retrace an old trip from my childhood days. I paddled off across the lake to an undeveloped shoreline, where I beached the canoe far back in the lily pads. Searching through the alder brush, I found an old trail that wound back through the woods to a 20-acre pond,

PREVIOUS PAGE: Birches glow on the shore of Blue Lake.
LEFT: A motorboat cuts through fog on Many Point Lake, near Detroit Lakes.
ABOVE: Red-necked grebes prowl the shallows of Potato Lake in Hubbard County.

with a big beaver dam at one end and high hills everywhere else. It looked just as it had years ago, when Dad and I carried a canoe back here and fished it for small bass and big bluegills. We called it Mud Lake, but no map I've ever seen has bothered to name it.

A couple of years ago, two friends and I hauled a canoe in to a certain Bass Lake at the end of a muddy and deeply rutted four-wheel-drive road. Though we didn't catch them that day, one of the fellows says he's caught a number of bass that were big—big enough to be ugly.

Over the years I have realized that you can find wild country in unexpected places. It may not be wilderness with a capital W. It may not qualify as a state park or a wild and scenic river. It may be one of the many, but relatively unvisited, state forests scattered around Minnesota. Or it may be nothing more than a few acres of woods that a road never reaches, or a strip of prairie along a railroad track, still untouched by the plow. But it's there, with enough untrammeled wildness and original character about it to tickle my imagination.

When I go back to the cabin, one of my favorite trips is to paddle down Daggett Brook. There's nothing exceptional about this waterway. There are dozens more like it. But that, perhaps, is what makes it—and all the others—exceptional.

Daggett spills from our lake over a foot-high Works Progress Administration dam, then runs through upland woods and boggy lowlands for perhaps four miles before reaching another lake. Weyerhaeuser floated virgin red and white pine down the creek at the turn of the century, but there's little evidence of that now. The clear water burbles over sand and beds of clams as thick as gravel on a road. A few cabins sit on its banks, but for the most part a canoe carries you around the bend and into solitude.

Daggett is where I learned to fly fish. Dad would bring me to a deep bend below the dam. Wearing shorts and tennis shoes, I waded into the upper end of the pool until I could feel the cool current push gently on my legs. Then I'd shake line through the guides of his old bamboo fly rod, work the line back and forth through the air and lay a tiny popper onto the limpid pool. I couldn't cast very well, but Daggett was a forgiving stream. The current straightened the fly line, carrying the popper to the deepest part of the hole. Sunfish and rock bass rose to the hook in splashy strikes. I played them, then released them once again to the current. It was art, as far as I'm concerned—the balance of color, motion, light, and shadow that gave form to my thoughts and desires. By catching a fish, I somehow captured the beauty of the moment. Art, like angling, is a matter of possession.

Daggett continues to enchant me. As I paddle downstream, mallards explode from the water and charge down river. A kingfisher chatters. A great

ABOVE: Ripples distort the reflection of aspen.
RIGHT: New leaves cover the trees in Mille Lacs Kathio State Park.
OVERLEAF: Wind sculpts drifted snow on Lake Lida, near Pelican Rapids.

blue heron squawks and flies around the next bend, to be flushed again and again. Once, while drifting on the easy current and not paying much attention, I ran my canoe into the bank. As I looked up I saw, within a foot of my canoe, a tiny fawn, frozen with indecision.

They say you can't step into the same river twice. That much is true. I can't see the lake and the stream and the cabin and my parents with the same eyes now. They have changed, and so have I. Yet I have discovered a way to appreciate these things with the same excitement I had as a child.

I have a photo on my wall. It shows my daughter, Kate. She is about four, and she is standing in the very spot where I used to fish. She is landing a sunfish on a small fly rod I made for her. As I look at this photo, I think of this unexceptional place where one life recapitulates another in the context of a living stream. Perhaps I can't step into the same river twice. Someone must wade in for me.

I think, too, of the power of wild country. This river—indeed this land of lakes like jewels, prairies and bogs, spirits and sky—has provided a path for my own life and now for my daughter's. Someday I will pass on, and so will she. Yet I hope this land remains forever wild.

LEFT: Red sumac grows on the shore of Mantrap Lake, near Akeley.
OVERLEAF: The sun sets on Burntside Lake.